I0541951

RAT
RACE
REBOOT

UNLOCK
YOUR FULL
POTENTIAL
TO ACHIEVE
IMPOSSIBLE
GOALS

LAURA NOEL

RAT RACE REBOOT
Unlock your full potential to achieve impossible goals
BY LAURA NOEL

Copyright © 2022 Laura Noel

Cover design and interior layout by
Yvonne Parks | PearCreative.ca

ISBN: 979-8-9859652-8-5

DEDICATION

I am in deep gratitude to my loving husband, Gary Noel, for his love and support throughout our life adventure together.

I am incredibly grateful to PSI seminars, the Hawaii Ohana and Margaret Zimmer for inspiring me to invest in my personal development.

I am sending much love to Bob Proctor, Sandy Gallagher, and the Proctor Gallagher Institute. You inspired me to go for my dreams and create the paradigm shift necessary to live them.

Thank you to Peggy McColl, who planted the seed and helped me see myself as an author; I am grateful for your support and mentorship.

Katie Boyd and Shirley Jump, this book would not have come to life without you, and I am so thankful for you!

Thank you to all of my Stretch Into Success clients from around the world for trusting me, gracing me with your presence, sharing your unique talents and gifts with the world, and showing up for your dreams in a big way!

Anik Singal and the LURN Center, a transformational place for Entrepreneurs, thank you for helping me expand my coaching business and enabling me to realize my vision.

Most of all, thank you to my loving parents, who taught me that I was capable of doing and being anything I truly wanted..

CONTENTS

DISCLAIMER

The advice and strategies found within may not be suitable for every situation. This work is sold with the understanding that neither the author nor the publisher are held responsible for the results accrued from the advice in this book.

INTRODUCTION

Are you always doing more and achieving more, yet still feeling like you aren't getting anywhere? Are you struggling to advance your goals while balancing all that with a life you love? Most of all, do you feel like you "should" be happy, but you aren't? Welcome to the rat race, where we are always running through the same maze and expecting a different outcome.

This is not how life is supposed to be. You're meant for much greater things than getting up, trudging to the office, putting your nose to the grindstone, and juggling a life, family, and hobbies while never feeling like anything is getting your full attention. The rat race is designed to keep you working toward some invisible (and impossible) finish line while making you feel like you are missing out on the sweetest moments in your life. You're pulled in a hundred directions.

That was me. I was the very definition of an overachiever who rose through the ranks in the military, competed in marathons and triathlons, and hit every target set in front of me. I was a workaholic who was desperately unhappy with my life. That's when I decided to step out of the rat race and rethink how I lived my life.

It took some detours and a few bumps in the road for me to learn how to let go of the person I used to be, fully embrace who I was meant to be, and realize that by living more fully and more *intentionally*, I could do less and achieve more. I went from someone who worked from sunup to sundown to becoming an Executive Business and Personal Development Consultant, tripling my level of income while working only four days a week. I have time to enjoy my life, take vacations, and also achieve my business and personal goals.

I dared to dream of that impossible goal and discovered the secrets behind making it happen. My mentor, the late and amazing Bob Proctor, helped push me in the right direction, and I wrote this book to help give you a nudge toward your own goals. Inside the pages of *Rat Race Reboot*, you'll find everything you need to know to finally get out of the rat race and live the life of your dreams.

We'll talk about the excuses that the world, your paradigms, and other people have thrown at you to keep you where you're at, then go through the solutions for reaching that next level, and finally, discuss the secret to making it all work for a lifetime.

Nothing happens overnight, so be prepared to do some mental work and start taking the reins of your destiny. The good news is that everything you need is already right here, in your hands and in your mind. You need to bring your mental, emotional, and physical game together. When you do that, you'll see powerful results and ask yourself why you waited so long to take the leap.

So turn the page and be prepared to say goodbye to the rat race. Whatever you dream can come true because everything is created twice—once in your imagination and once in physical form. Let's get started!

PART ONE
THE EXCUSES

CHAPTER 1

KNOW WHAT YOU WANT

The conference room is full of excuses, and every one of them is something I have heard before. The Owner/CEO and his team of vice presidents are trying to explain to me why the business isn't reaching the next level while I listen and take notes, all part of the intake process. It doesn't matter what the excuses are because they all boil down to the same thing—something external is preventing the business from growing.

Those external influences, however, are not the true cause of the company's struggles. They're also not part of the solutions. If that sounds like a whole different way of looking at your company, it is, and if you can shift the way you think about challenges and success, you can shift the trajectory of your future. How? Well, you have to understand how the mind works before changing how it impacts you.

So many of the people I work with struggle with their businesses and their lives. They feel like they're stretched in ten different directions while simultaneously trying to tread water in rough seas. They are usually effective in some areas, but not all, and the constant juggling act is exhausting them, their teams, and their businesses.

If you think this doesn't apply to you, first ask yourself a few questions: Are you working incredibly hard but at the expense of having the life you wanted when you first started out? Are you constantly trying to catch up on the important details of your life? Are you putting yourself last on the list over and over again? Are you missing the soccer games and saying no to spontaneous vacations with a loved one?

ARE YOU STRUGGLING TO BALANCE IT ALL?

The months of quarantine during Covid-19 gave many people a wake-up call. They were at home for weeks at a time and suddenly realized how much they were missing out on by pouring everything they had into their businesses—and despite those efforts, they were still not moving the company ball forward at the pace they wanted. They were on a hamster wheel that wasn't going anywhere, and those futile efforts were costing them valuable time with their loved ones. As life returned to normal and business owners returned to their offices, those realizations became even stronger.

The first question I ask an entrepreneur or CEO is a simple one on its surface, but ultimately, these few words delve into many complicated issues.

WHAT IS HOLDING YOU BACK?

The answers vary and run the gamut of things like *I'm working on this project. I don't know which opportunity to pursue because I don't want to lose out. I don't want to let people down. My team isn't on board. I don't have the capital to expand. My spouse doesn't support me. I don't have enough time to do this.*

I understand. Before I started this book, I was working full-time as a business coach and pursuing my doctorate. Full-time school, full-time work. Where was I going to find the time? But I knew the book was critical to my work and helping my clients, so I found a way to manage my time and make this a priority.

Everyone can relate to not having enough time, people, or capital to do what they need to. These are the typical excuses I hear for not reaching one's full potential. My answer? It's far easier to focus on all these things outside your control than on the one thing that is in your control: *You*.

If you're stalling in your growth or overwhelmed and frustrated, chances are good that the root cause is already inside you; it's part of your built-in paradigm. I'm not saying you're being lazy or unfocused. Quite the opposite. The typical Type-A people I speak with are all programmed to work hard. However, in the quest to do more, be better, earn more, etc., we are working with old, tired programming. That hypnotic grind of the hustle culture that got you where you are today has become who you are. It's a part of your identity or self-image. It's also created other problems.

Einstein said, "We cannot solve our problems using the same thinking we used when we created them." Typically, when people want to level up in all areas of their lives, they do more of the same. That makes sense, but it also doesn't in another way because no matter how much "success" you have, you're still stuck in this self-imposed trap of doing more, being better, earning more, etc. You can't outperform your self-image or your self-beliefs. It's like holding the brake down while you're gunning the engine with the other foot—no matter how hard you work, your progress will be impacted. You may feel like you're achieving, and you probably are, but you're not achieving as big as you could.

ARE YOU PLAYING SMALL?

Type-A people are the ones who run that hamster wheel at warp speed. They are driven, which makes them work extra hard. They often achieve high levels of success and win awards, and then go after even more. But chances are good that they're also playing small in the game of life and career.

Playing small means not reaching your full potential. You're settling for wins but not going after the super-big, super-scary goals, the ones you could shoot for—and possibly not obtain. We are as afraid of failure as we are of success, and that subconscious thinking keeps us stuck in neutral.

Everything we have right this minute has been manifested by our subconscious thinking. That old saying attributed to Buddha, "What you think, you become," is true. You are thinking small, and therefore your results are small.

Your results may be incredibly impressive from the outside looking in, and you should be proud of your accomplishments. But, are you being left with this nagging feeling that you could be doing more or that you were put here on this earth for a higher purpose? That there is so much more you could do, with far less effort than you are currently expending? How would it feel to get ten times the results and work half the time, knowing you are confidently and quickly making the right decisions and leveraging the right opportunities, ultimately living your best life?

WHAT WOULD HAPPEN IF YOU STARTED THINKING BIG?

We'll get to how you think big in a minute. First, I want to explain how this works because I saw it firsthand in my own life.

During my military career, I made it to the top 1% of the enlisted force and was very successful, earning six figures and outperforming many of my colleagues. I was in that top percentile, even as a woman in a male-dominated world. When I joined the Air Force, I had a huge chip on my shoulder and often pushed back on authority. My image of what a leader was and what a leader looked like was the stereotypical boisterous domineering man, a hardcover extrovert— the exact opposite of me.

My mentors were pushing me to take on leadership roles, but that paradigm about leadership was deeply ingrained. They saw a potential in me that I couldn't see in myself. Even though other people were pushing me to grow, and I had overcome enormous obstacles to get where I was, I subconsciously held myself back. It wasn't until much later that I realized that paradigm was blocking me from moving forward and taking those risks.

Paradigm : par·a·digm | \ ˈper-ə-ˌdīm , ˈpa-rə- also -ˌdim \

Definition of *paradigm*

1: example, pattern especially: an outstandingly clear or typical example or archetype … *regard science as the paradigm of true knowledge.* — G. C. J. Midgley

2: an example of a conjugation or declension showing a word in all its inflectional forms

3: a philosophical and theoretical framework of a scientific school or discipline within which theories, laws, and generalizations and the experiments performed in support of them are formulated. broadly: a philosophical or theoretical framework of any kind

Source: Merriam-Webster Online Dictionary

It wasn't until I decided to dive deep into those inner beliefs that I began to see that I was holding onto self-limiting beliefs (the paradigms that formed the limits in my mind, in other words). I began working with Bob Proctor and a mastermind group to peel back those layers of thoughts, and as I did, more and more opportunities opened up for me.

My mentor could see what I couldn't and helped open my eyes. As an outsider without any stake in the game, his point of view was different. It's the same as when I'm sitting in that conference room listening to the excuses and reasonings being bandied about by leadership. I hear and see things they can't because they are too close to the problem.

Changing my thinking changed my goals, and I began to reach for things that seemed impossible, like being promoted to E-9/Chief Senior Master Sergeant. My attitude changed, and I was asked to be a mentor to other women in the military and be the keynote speaker at various events and the Airmen Leadership School.

I began reaching out to other women at the same level in the military and created a networking group. When I was in Hawaii at the Military Professional Education Center, I set up a meeting with the other women at a nearby restaurant. The commandant of the education center and I were the first to arrive. As we chatted, she told me she was taking another post and encouraged me to apply for her job.

My first instinct was to say no. At the time, I was the band manager for the regional Air Force band in the Pacific and had gone through years of disregard by other people over my role in the military. People would say that it was the band, not the real military, and therefore not as real or as difficult or as important. For many years, I had allowed myself to be impacted by these social judgments and would turn down opportunities like this one. I had let what I was brought up to believe, and other people's opinions control my destiny for too long.

Instead, I said, "I'll apply for that." The next day I called our Air Force personnel center and said I wanted to apply for the job. They told me I couldn't because the window for applying had just closed.

In my head and my gut, I knew I could handle this job, and I saw myself in the role, even though there was no way to put my name in front of the people who did the hiring. Instead of being defeated, I was restructuring that leadership paradigm in my head by concentrating on my belief that I could do this—and would.

I kept calling the personnel office. "Hi, it's Chief Noel. I know you said no, but is there any way I can apply for the commandant position anyway?" They finally told me to call my command in the Pacific and ask them about applying. When I did, the woman on the other end of the phone sighed. "Ma'am, that ad has been closed for fourteen days. You can't apply."

I called the Air Force personnel office again, and once again, they told me no. "Thank you," I said, "But I've decided I'm going to apply anyway. I feel it, I want it, and I'm the right person for this job."

I had to jump through hoops to get a letter of recommendation from my boss, who was in the middle of a move, and then get my application sent in. Every step seemed impossible, and I had a dozen roadblocks to navigate, but I did everything I could to get my resume on the right desk, then went on a much-needed vacation while I was on leave. Everyone told me there was no way I could get a job that had already been closed to new applications, but I knew that position would be mine. I didn't know how; I just believed in myself and my impossible goal.

The day I returned from my cruise, I got a phone call from the command chief. "Congratulations, Chief Noel," he said. "You got the job, and you start next month."

I was surprised, but also not, even though the impossible had just come true. I didn't know at the time that there was a whole chain of events happening in the background while I just kept on believing and pushing forward. A series of serendipitous or universe-created events (however you want to look at it) was part of what brought my belief into a reality.

Just as everyone said, the Air Force *had* hired someone else to replace the departing commandant, but the new hire was offered another position elsewhere at the same time. She chose to go to that post instead of the Hawaii post. That left the assignment open again.

That keynote speech I had given months earlier at the Airmen Leadership School was one of the most nerve-wracking things I'd ever done, but it was also part of my journey to overcome those self-limiting beliefs. I had no idea that the incoming command chief and the commander for the base would be there as well. We were seated at the head table, and they saw me in action, inspiring and taking charge of the room. When my application came across their desk, they remembered me and already knew I could handle the job.

> There were a million reasons I shouldn't have gotten that job, but I did. Changing that paradigm meant I could reach for skies that had seemed impossible to reach before. I thought big, believed big, and refused to play small. I've applied those lessons to every segment of my life ever since, and it's helped me create the life I dreamed of back when I was a kid in Lancaster, PA.

If you want a future of unlimited possibilities, great. Those doors don't just magically open because you want them to. You can't have any of this if you can't dream it, so that's where you start.

WHAT DO YOU WANT?

If you could wave a magic wand and have the life you always dreamed of, what would that look like? Most people rattle off a salary that would make their dreams come true, but it goes deeper than what's in your bank account.

There are three core things that people want:

1. Not necessarily to be rich but to have enough money to live exactly as they want and to be free from the worry about finances. Essentially, the financial freedom to go on that impromptu trip, buy the golf clubs, pay for the kids' college, etc.

2. To be surrounded by and have relationships with upbeat individuals who are enthusiastic about life and encourage creativity in those they know.

3. To wake up every day enthused about the day ahead.

And then there is one deeper thing that many of us don't realize is at the base of everything we do. We want to serve at our highest potential. People want to know that what they do matters and land on that thing that makes a difference, a thing that they also love doing.

They want to have a job that doesn't feel like working instead of a daily grind of commutes and frustrations. They want to come home to the people they love happy and fulfilled so that they give their loved ones the best of themselves.

So let's go back to that question. ***What do you want?***

I want you to close your eyes and really picture this life. Where are you living? How big is your house? What are you driving? Where do you go on vacation? What fills your weekends? Who is surrounding you? What does your life *feel* like?

Keep thinking about and picturing this life until it's as real as the chair you are sitting in or the ground under your feet. Imagine a life bigger and better than any you have imagined before. Do you crave that life? Can you feel that need deep inside yourself?

Good. Because that's an emotional connection, and that's key to change. If you just set incremental goals like "I want to go to Colorado next spring," then you aren't emotionally connected. Sure, you want to go to Colorado, but you don't have this soul-deep need to go there. However, if you set a big, huge, scary, exciting goal that is tied to your heart—say, travel the entire world with your kids before you turn fifty—then you create an emotional connection.

It doesn't matter if what you're dreaming of seems illogical or impossible. We've been taught to be logical and to stay within the fences of what's already set before us. I'm asking you to go further than that. To shoot for the grass way behind the Big Green Monster at Fenway.

Except . . . here's the problem with paradigms. You can dream all you want, but when you start stretching in new, big, scary ways, your paradigm will yank you right back. It's similar to how your body seems to feel every ache and pain just before you lace up your running shoes. Your body is saying, *no way, you can't do this, it's too hard, you better go back to the couch*. I've had to overcome that thinking dozens of times, and make it through tough races like the Kona Ironman. To achieve something like that, you have to shut off the part of your brain that says *I can't do this*. It's the same with these scary goals.

Your big goal isn't the same as anyone else's big goal, either. You might not dream of owning a private jet; maybe you want to have a four-day work week or more time with your kids. Maybe you want to move to California, franchise your company, or retire at fifty. This is all about listening to your inner guidance and deciding what goals fit *you*—not what someone else thinks your goal should be.

I can tell you to change your mind, but it's not as easy as that. There are only two ways our paradigms get shifted:

1. An Emotional Earthquake: This is an event that shakes you to the core and makes you change on the spot. A brush with death, a major heart attack, the loss of someone dear. That trauma can force change because the emotional impact has become impressed on your subconscious mind.

2. A Mindset Reset: Most of us exist in our comfort zones quite happily. Our minds are trained to stay there in that safe, snuggly space. To force a change, you have to reset your mindset, and you do that pretty much like you train a puppy— with time, space, repetition, and accountability with a coach.

Everything is created first in our minds, and only then can it manifest in a physical form. You have to believe before you receive, to paraphrase Mom's words about Santa. This book is here to help you do that and develop the skillset you need to change.

HOW COMMITTED ARE YOU TO CHANGING?

I deal with smart people every day who are stuck in the mud, not because they don't have the degrees and accolades to move forward but because their limiting beliefs are more powerful than their desire for more. These highly successful people feel guilty and ashamed because they feel they should know better and do better. What they aren't seeing is the gap between knowing and doing.

In school, no one teaches us to make decisions based on what we want instead of on our reality. My reality was that the job wasn't meant to be because they were already closed to new applications. The old me would have just gone on vacation and stayed in the job I had. Instead, I went with what I believed in—even though many people told me it was impossible—and saw it happen.

Remember when you first learned to ride a bike? Riding without training wheels and balancing on two thin tires seemed impossible. To learn, you had to have faith in yourself, in the bike, and in the process, and you had to take the risk of riding without a safety net.

Your paradigms will always win and pull you back to reality if you don't have a clear picture of the future you want and if you aren't deeply in love with that future and what it represents. Part Two will help you set those goals, and Part Three will help you execute them. For now, I want you to just start thinking about the world beyond those mental fences.

CHAPTER 2

ACT AS IF YOU'RE EFFICIENT

When Bob Proctor, the speaker and thought leader, was working at Prudential Insurance, he met a guy who had been with the company for twenty-two years. The other man pointed out an award and said, "I've always wanted to earn one of those awards."

The company had many programs to give away awards in several different categories. This guy had been a mid-level performer and had what it took to receive an award, but Bob could tell the real problem behind his empty shelf was having the wrong priorities in his thinking. "You've been trying this for twenty-two years, and it hasn't worked because you are violating Universal Laws by trying to 'get,'" Bob told him.

He explained to the other man that the only way to achieve what you want is to see yourself as the kind of person who is at that level. As we discussed in the previous chapter, you have to believe that you are that person. That extends to all parts of your work and regular life. We keep wasting time wanting to be there instead of using our time to get there.

But what if you don't believe it yet or aren't quite there yet? The man knew he deserved an award but couldn't quite see himself receiving one. Bob told him that wanting something wasn't enough. It's the difference between an actor who just reads his lines and one who *becomes* the character. When you are living the role, you easily become that person.

When I was transitioning out of the military and becoming an entrepreneur, I had to change from wearing combat boots to designer suits. Every time I got dressed, I kept reminding myself of who I wanted to be. In my imagination, I was a successful businesswoman who made the most of her time, freedom, and philanthropy. But in my current physical reality during the work week, I was an Airman serving my country and needing to get vacation time approved if I wanted to travel somewhere.

On the weekends, I would dress like that person I saw in my imagination. I'd put on the suits I couldn't wear in the military and physically shift into the entrepreneur I was on my way to being. I had a screen saver image on my computer of the non-profit organization I wanted to help. I acted *as if* I was that person, and all these seemingly little things I did added up until that was who I became. I believed it, and that reality unfolded for me.

If you're not quite ready to make a big paradigm shift, try a smaller one. For example, I had a friend who was training for a race and wanted to eat much healthier. He would ask himself before every meal, "How would an athlete fuel his body?" He started acting as if he was that endurance athlete he wanted to be with every choice he made, and before he knew it, he was one.

TOSS, CHANGE, OR KEEP?

If you were a person who managed their time successfully, what would that life look like? Would you have reached a certain milestone financially, or would you be efficient enough in your work life to have plenty of time with your family to go on regular vacations? Just as you did for the first chapter, I want you to imagine living a life of successful activity management. Maybe that means you exercise right after you get up or clear up your entire to-do list when you're at work. Perhaps that means getting things off of your calendar altogether by delegating or—gasp—actually saying *no*.

What are the profit-earning activities in your business, what parts of your business do you enjoy doing, and what do you dread doing? Make a list and then find the people to fill in the blanks so you can do things like leaving early enough to eat dinner with your kids or taking your partner to a movie. Whatever successful time management means to you, I want you to close your eyes and see yourself doing exactly that.

When I speak to corporate clients, I have them go through the same exercise, only for their company. I ask them the same simple question—one that exposes complicated layers underneath the company's struggles:

If an outside consultant were to come in and look at the time spent in your business on various activities, would they say the team was efficient? If not, then where is everyone's energy and time being drained?

Have your team members do this exercise individually, and you may uncover some problems that may surprise you. Then ask yourself where you would rather see your team spending their time. What activities do team members feel would create the best results and momentum? Asking your team this question can create a great flow of ideas.

When the CEO or management team gives this question real thought, it helps them discern what needs to shift or change, or what processes to revamp. They see the lost hours in processing paperwork, the people who aren't in jobs that suit their best skills, or the Monday morning quarterbacking that doesn't institute real change.

It's like standing in your kitchen and dreaming of the perfect work and cook space for your busy family. Thousands of homeowners renovate their kitchens every year, not just to update but to improve the efficiency of this space they enter at least three times a day. *Architectural Digest* recently ran an article on the importance of the "working triangle" in a kitchen. This concept, developed in the twentieth century, is based on the theory that the three main work areas in the kitchen—sink, refrigerator, and stove—should form a triangle for best efficiency. The legs of the triangle should be between four and nine feet in length, and the sum distance of the triangle should be no less than thirteen feet and no more than twenty-six feet. Any smaller, and you create bottlenecks when you're cooking or cleaning up. Any larger, and you're wasting precious time getting from one area to the next.

When you look at your business, where are your wasted time areas and your bottlenecks? There are reasons behind the time management choices you have made, which we'll get into later in the book, but for now, I just want you to list the areas where you or your company are the least efficient.

As you would with a kitchen renovation, I want you to think about what you would toss, keep, or change in your business. What things drain your energy? What things are wasting your time? Which things are keeping you from living that life you dreamed about? Don't worry about being perfect here—your goal is to get this down on paper so you can give it an objective look.

Deciding on which things you need to let go of consists of a simple two-question checklist:

1. Is this no longer my priority?
2. Is this serving the forward momentum of myself, my employees, or my business?

You can say all day long that you want to be a more efficient person or company, but that's not the same as being one right *now*. You can't espouse values that you aren't living and demonstrating. Your culture must match the way you operate. Not there yet? Go back to Proctor's advice and act as if you are. That old "fake it till you make it" saying is popular because it's true. If you act like a person who is efficient and living the dream, you will become one in your habitual actions.

However, there is one caveat: when you take actions "as if" you are that person, you are creating the paradigm shift and belief at the same time—but only if you truly feel that as if person in your bones. Without believing and feeling like you are that person, the old "fake it till you make it" won't work.

THE TIME SUCKERS

In my years of work in corporate structures and with corporate clients, I have seen several common areas of time wasting. These are part of companies big and small, in pretty much every industry, including the military, which is essentially the largest business in the United States. There's a reason the Kellogg School of Management at Northwestern University has an Army Colonel speak to their school every year—the military has figured out how to implement the systems and strategies that keep it humming along.[1] But just as with any other giant corporation, there are areas that challenge its efficiency.

1. Micromanaging:

I was in an organization within the military where the entire atmosphere was very authoritarian. All the decisions were made by the leader and no one else, and any creativity or expertise was immediately squashed. Every single thing the team tried to implement was squashed by the top, either by second-guessing or micromanaging.

Micromanaging comes from a lack of trust and an innate insecurity. Managers who feel the necessity to handle every single thing in their department often feel like no one else can do their job the way they do it or that they will become nonessential the second they let someone else take charge. They feel a deep need to get outside validation of their worth and success. Many micromanagers know they are taking on more than they should and are paying their price in stress and overwhelm, but the payoff is an easy win, and not having to work through the fear of giving up control.

---

1   Take 5: What Business Leaders Can Learn from the Military," Kellogg Insight, September 25, 2020. https://insight. kellogg.northwestern.edu/article/business-lessons-from-military.

2. *Waffling on Decisions*:

As children, we're not taught how to make decisions. We're taught to be information gatherers, to collect data until we feel we have enough to make the best choice. The problem? We get analysis paralysis. We are bombarded with information in this digital age—more than we have ever had access to—and it creates an inability to make a choice, which makes us waste time waffling back and forth. Or worse yet, we keep asking others what we should do, which means we are looking outside ourselves for answers. Knowing more doesn't necessarily mean we will do more.

The same thing happens when a leader goes into a meeting and asks for opinions and lets everyone talk in an endless circle of options. If you are clear on what you want and get input from others, you can quickly decide whether it will work and then *move forward.* If you aren't clear, you become indecisive, using the excuse of waiting on data. There will never be enough data for you to be confident in your decisions. Never. Just make a decision and take action. Failure is feedback, not a stopping point.

3. *Lacking Clarity*:

We talked about this in Chapter One. If you aren't clear on what you want or where you want to be, you're wasting time taking detours. You have to know what you want and have that vision in your mind all the time, so every move you make brings you closer to that vision.

4. *Being Busy for the Sake of Being Busy*:

Today's world is like a rushing river—everyone's doing something all the time, which makes people feel like they are wasting time if they are just standing on the banks, thinking and planning their next move. It's a common misconception that being busy equals being productive. It isn't.

Being productive means that everything you put your time into is moving you forward. Simply being busy means you are moving laterally—or not moving forward. It's like sitting in the car and fiddling with the radio or adjusting the seat instead of driving. You're busy—but you're not going anywhere.

5. *Letting the Past Define the Future*:

Organizations that are setting goals or milestones typically look at past projections or strategic plans as a benchmark. Then they usually choose to achieve the same goal or make an incremental gain. What if you instead, you made a goal based on what you truly want and desire? What if you choose to focus on that ultimate dream life instead of past results?

Looking at past results to drive our thinking doesn't generate that emotional need to achieve more because we stay stuck in the past, recreating the same results. Staying stuck in the past doesn't allow you to see the possibility of expansion and something greater. We need to create that urgent feeling that moves the body to action by using our higher mental faculties: imagination, intuition, reason, memory, will, and perception.

6. Getting Stuck in the How:

Just like analysis paralysis, worrying about how we will achieve a goal often keeps us from even attempting to go after it. Reframing and leading individuals or teams through the process of reframing is and always will be a part of my tool kit. The piece many of us miss when we do this is the "why" that makes reframing so effective.

Hebb's law says that neurons that fire together wire together. When our amygdala is activated, and we feel stuck in a circumstance (and as a result, we start suppressing stress so we can focus on the problem), we aren't thinking or responding; we are reacting.[2] However, we have the ability to override the mental programming that keeps us stuck in less productive, habitual patterns and ways of thinking. We can do this through the practice of reframing, which is about seeing the challenge from another perspective and creating a new model.

Overthinking and overreliance on the rational mind can dampen the impact of our intuitive judgments. Our moods can impact our ability to access our innate wisdom, particularly when trying to understand others.[3] To access that creativity within our unconscious mind, we need to get proper rest, have fun, and exercise. Last week, I felt overwhelmed and, consequently, spiraled into a crappy mood. I only saw problems and was blind to my creative power and intuitive wisdom. When I walked away, reframed the situation, and took a nap, I woke up with a fresh perspective and a great solution.

I remember having meetings addressing KPIs; if one of us hadn't met a target, we were held accountable. We

2   Collins, Stella. Neuroscience for Learning and Development: How to Apply Neuroscience and *Psychology for Improved Learning and Training*. 2nd ed. Kogan Page, 2019.

3   Ghadiri, Argang, Andreas Habermacher, and Theo Peters. (2012). Neuroleadership: A journey through the brain for business leaders, Springer, 2012.

took responsibility and personal accountability, and the entire team encouraged, supported, and strategized. We were invested in being our best, making everyone more efficient.

> The best companies I have worked with have encouraged creativity, taking risks, making mistakes, and stretching the envelope a little bit further. They don't get stuck in the past; instead, they let people work from that place of hunger deep inside them.

You can find and foster creative thinking anywhere, in any organization. For instance, when I was a Master Sergeant and part of the Air Force Regional band, we opted to form a small rock band that would dress in civilian clothes and play at different schools. We were thinking outside the box to gain access to schools and organizations that normally didn't welcome the military. In turn, we were bridging the gap and fostering relationships. The music we played shifted the energy in the group and in the room, and our camaraderie as a group was through the roof. We were emotionally invested in the success because we weren't micromanaged or stuck in analysis—we were going with our guts and being creative in our approach.

No matter how technical your field is, start making a change by giving yourself permission to get out of the weeds and stop wasting time on things that keep you mired in the status quo. Allow yourself the freedom to think in new ways, and you'll find that energy you need.

Enthusiasm and excitement are great propellants. They create that emotional investment that helps people manage their time better and keep moving the ball forward. Keep the ultimate goal on your vision board. Have your team see it every single day, so they are constantly envisioning that future you have dreamed of. Define it, imagine it, and focus on it.

AVOIDING THE GOAL HANGOVER

No matter how big or small your team is, at some point you will inevitably experience a goal dip, a sort of hangover that can become a roadblock if you don't know how to overcome it. You're moving forward, making progress, and moving fast, then suddenly, your mind starts telling you it's a fluke. It's not going to happen again. You're aiming too high.

None of that is true. It's the whispers of your old paradigms, trying to keep you safe and secure in the status quo. In essence, your mind hasn't caught up with your abilities.

A dip always accompanies that progressive realization of a worthy ideal, especially when we reach something bigger than we originally thought we could. Maybe your sales goal was set at $100,000 for the first quarter, and at the end of March, you realize you have hit $200,000 in sales. You have that adrenaline high—then the crash, where you're thinking, "Oh shit, now what? Am I equipped to handle this next level?"

Yes, you are. If you have imagined a goal, then it's yours to have. Your intuition guides you in those intentions, and that inner sensibility is something greater than yourself.

> If you can believe it and see it in your mind, you can achieve it.

Most of us get in our own way and don't realize we are experiencing a subtle form of self-sabotage, or we get stuck listening to our inner critic and back away from challenges. We don't understand that those paradigms and inner self-image obstructions are getting in the way. The bigger your success, the louder and more strident your paradigm will be. It manifests in sleepless nights, crankiness, anxiety, and overthinking.

You have to realize those fears are simply a natural step in the process. Don't waste time looking backward. Just acknowledge the fear, feel it fully and completely for a moment, and then *choose* to move forward and not engage with those inner doubts any longer.

If you don't, you are wasting time by dwelling in that fear of the very success you want and desire. You're allowing the paradigm to drive you instead of choosing to drive yourself. The next few chapters will give you concrete tips on how to do less worrying and more thinking and acting.

PROCRASTINATION CAN SHOW UP AS FEAR

I've met dozens of people who tell me they are chronic procrastinators. One woman I know was highly successful in her field and knew she could achieve ten times what she had done thus far. But she kept herself stuck by procrastinating on the very things that could get her to that next level. She told me it was a bad habit she'd developed when she was in college and overwhelmed by her course load. "It's just part of who I am," she said. "I can't change it." But when we looked at her tendency to put things off in more detail, she realized that fear of success (as well as the responsibility of success and inner pressure to not let people down), not a habit, was at the root of her problems. In other words, she was experiencing imposter syndrome.

Go back to that list of time wasters, and you'll find many of the symptoms of procrastination there. Procrastination can take many forms, from continuing to gather data for days on end to being overly busy to bingeing Netflix for hours, procrastination can take many forms. It looks different to each individual—find out what form procrastination takes for you.

The people who are busy all day believe they are moving forward, but they really aren't. They are chipping away at small goals and avoiding the big ones they need to tackle. If you procrastinate by watching television, quitting cold turkey likely won't work. You have consciously replaced that behavior with something else. Your paradigms guide 96 to 98% of our habitual behaviors; if you don't consciously choose, then the paradigm will choose for you. Chances are, the paradigm's option won't be the one you want or need to make. Why? Because the paradigm's whole purpose is to keep you in that safe, comfy spot where you won't get hurt, you won't fail, and you also won't reach for the stars.

CHAPTER 3

OVERCOME YOUR "LACK" OF RESOURCES

If only we had _____, we could be successful/reach this level/be the best in our industry, etc.

I've heard the litany of limitations CEOs say are holding them back, and chances are that you have too or are saying them yourself. *If only* becomes a common theme in my coaching sessions. If only we had more resources—people, space, funding, M&Ms in the breakroom, whatever it is—we would be successful.

Here's the universal truth: You don't have a lack of resources. Instead, you have limitless abundance at your fingertips.

I know it sounds crazy, but trust me, your resources are there and always have been, because Einstein proved they were. Albert Einstein discovered that energy could not be destroyed; it could only be changed from one form to another. Ice becomes water, and water becomes ether. The H2O is still there, just in a different form. His groundbreaking scientific discovery is the secret to dreaming big.

The Laws of physics, including the Laws of Conservation of Mass and Energy that Einstein studied, prove that nothing is created or destroyed. Essentially, everything that ever was and ever will be exists right now.

How is that possible? Think about the cell phone you use every day, a thing that most of us couldn't even comprehend before it was invented. The technology for the cell phone has always been here and available to us. Yet, it wasn't until people *imagined the possibility* of having a small device in the palm of their hand that could reach any person in any part of the world at any time that these products seemed to appear out of the ether. The energy and resources were there—they just needed to be transformed and transmuted from an idea to a product.

Man is only limited by weakness of attention
and poverty of imagination.

NEVILLE GODDARD

Goddard says that we limit ourselves because we don't
dare to dream big. The truth is, there is an abundant
supply of everything we need to manufacture and
realize any dream. Instead of believing in that, we get
stuck in a mindset of scarcity.

I know that some companies experiencing growing
pains feel a pinch as they begin to expand and their
current resources are tested. That's a temporary state as
you figure out ways to make more of what you have.
I'm talking about a bigger-picture, overall sense of
scarcity that invades every decision and hinders growth.

The mind is a powerful thing. Advertisers have known
this for centuries. They are adept at making us feel
a sense of scarcity or a fear of missing out (FOMO)
because we don't have a Coach purse or drive a Land
Rover. We overextend our credit or hold ourselves back
from bigger things because we are afraid we don't have
enough "whatever" to get there.

To be in alignment with Universal Laws, we have to
reject that hypnotic grind of the hustle culture, aka

the rat race. If we want to stretch ourselves, we need to move from competition to a more creative and collaborative plane. To do that, we must shed the old paradigms and get behind the mantra: *Amateurs compete; professionals create.*

If you ask ten CEOs about the resources they think they lack, the answers will fall into a few categories:

1. *An Edge over the Competition*:

These people get caught up in always looking over their shoulder at the competition, which subconsciously gives them a mindset of lack and scarcity. If you are in this group, you probably find yourself working to put out fires and constantly shifting priorities. It will feel like you're running on a hamster wheel and getting nowhere. As a result, you and your team will feel exhausted and burned out.

Too many of us focus on trying to one-up the competition so we can get a piece of the pie, but we forget that the pie is unlimited. We are expending valuable mental energy on comparison instead of on creation, the only thing that can ultimately bring us that slice of pie.

In addition, when you focus on your competition, you tend to copy what they are doing instead of being unique to who you are. That's a different energy than the one you get when you focus on gleaning and implementing their best practices. Doing that builds on your creativity instead of keeping you mired in worry.

2. Intel on the Competition:

In Chapter Two, we talked about how endless data gathering becomes analysis paralysis. You'll never know everything about your competition, and you don't need to. Focusing on gathering intel on your competition is like stalking an ex on social media to find out who they're dating now. You're draining your current relationship or missing out on the perfect one because you are putting energy and focus on something that's in the past and out of your control.

Instead, you should be doing market research to know who you serve and what they want. Then you will be coming from a place of service (serving the end client), which is more about giving than getting. Those philosophies work with, not against, Universal Laws.

3. Creativity on the Team:

Every single one of us has God-given creativity. There's only one you—and you are unique. Collectively, the team has its unique creative spirit, too. Too often, we get caught up in comparison or focusing on the past. When you do that, as I mentioned earlier, *you're working on imitating, not creating.* Studying others can be a positive thing because it can draw out your own creativity. As you evolve from imitation to inspiration, you can make those new ideas work for you and the people you serve.

CREATE A PLACE FOR CREATIVITY

I periodically coach at the LURN center for entrepreneurs, and they showed me a room they called the Insane Asylum. The entire room was made of whiteboard, even the ceiling. They encouraged us to doodle, to let our creativity come out on those blank slates.

As adults, we refrain from doing those kinds of things, which seems crazy to me. Little kids learn about their world and their place in it by banging on pots and pans, writing on the wall, fingerpainting, and dozens of other creative outlets. Once we get to school, we're taught to stay within the box of our five senses. Sit down, pay attention, don't touch that, write this down, listen to me. Our sixth sense, the one full of innate abilities, imagination, intuition, reason, will, memory, and perception, ends up buried.

So go ahead, draw on the walls, see the refrigerator box as a fort, or just allow yourself space to imagine. Even better, create a space in your office for people to create and broaden their thinking!

When I was with the ground mobile radar unit, when a problem arose, we didn't have time to keep looking at the past or at what other people were doing outside of our team. We had to work together to look forward, and then move forward. Being stuck in bewilderment, confusion, or stagnation can be a life-or-death situation in the military. If any of us was stuck in bewilderment and comparison, people's lives could be lost.

The stakes may not be as high for your business, but the same principles apply—trust in the unique creativity your team is already blessed with. Give them the space and time to dream big and dream of the impossible.

If a member of the team is struggling to see the vision or to trust that it can happen, sometimes they need to be reassigned, and sometimes they just need to be coaxed to open their minds. When you start doing this work and understanding mindset and Universal Laws, you start to understand others and what makes them tick.

I don't think people choose to go to work and do a horrible job and undermine progress. Very often, it's their paradigm, their fears, and their limiting beliefs that keep them from performing their best. When that happens, have them do the exercises you have done in this book.

Or call a team meeting, and ask them: If we were in a world without bureaucracy, policies, or limitations to trip us up, what would we be doing right now? What could we create? How high could we reach? Let them see the possibilities and get emotionally attached to the outcome. Then you have the investment of your most important resource—your team.

4. Not Enough Funding/Space/Time:

These all fall into the same category. We all go through times when we feel like we don't have enough of what we need to finish a job or to expand. The problem isn't with the square footage in your building—it's in your *mindset*.

When you hesitate and don't trust your intuition and your higher self, accounts are lost, opportunities are lost, and relationships are lost. Why? Because you are looking outside yourself for resources and direction.

You have essentially closed off your mind to seeing the possibilities, so you can't see the brilliance of partnering with a vendor to build a JIT (Just In Time) inventory space or creating a collaborative team with another business. We close off our minds by subconsciously telling our reticular activating system that we want to see more obstacles. If that's what you put out there, that's what you will see.

Get quiet, open your mind, and allow yourself to believe all those things are already there, waiting for you to invite them into your world. The people, the time, the funding—it's there if you trust Universal Laws. When you start to listen to and hear your inner GPS, you have no choice but to follow it because that visceral gut instinct, which is very often right, is driving you. This is a learned skill I will teach you as we move through the book.

5. Support from Others:

Whether it's support from shareholders, your team, or your family, many of us can see a quiet cheering section as a reason to stay where we are. Their lack of support is not something that's inside your control. It's their own paradigms in place, their own biases from their experiences.

The most inventive people in the world were considered crazy by the people around them. Imagine Benjamin Franklin's family watching him go out in a thunderstorm in 1752 to fly a kite attached to a jar fitted with conducting wires. Lightning was striking, and Franklin was trying to capture this incredible force of nature to study it. To outsiders, Franklin was insane. This man, who invented stoves and swim fins, bifocals and batteries, allowed himself to imagine the possibilities and to trust in the Universal Laws. He knew the technology was there—he just needed to capture and work with it.

We think things into existence. Ponder on that for a second. Someone thought of the cell phone, and it became a thing. Someone thought of a battery, and it was created. Someone thought of the internet, and it was born. They persisted until it existed.

Care shouldn't start in the emergency room.

JAMES DOUGLAS

When we become emotionally involved in our ideas, that strengthens our belief we can have them. It becomes the fuel that drives our actions. That internal GPS—your visceral gut instinct—guides you in taking the biggest risks or developing the most inventive solutions.

There are creative options for even the most complicated problems. I knew an OEM manufacturer who had a huge opportunity with Ford. They were awarded a contract to produce parts for every single Ford vehicle—a massive opportunity that would take that little company to a whole new level. The problem? Their plant wasn't big enough to produce that many parts, and the transportation costs would be prohibitive. Their solution was genius (and is something used by many other OEM manufacturers today)—build a small temporary building beside the Ford plant and manufacture the parts there as they are needed, a JIT inventory solution that no one had done before.

CHANGE YOUR SPACE TO CHANGE YOUR MINDSET

Don't get to the point of losing your business before you start changing your mindset and learning to work with Universal Laws. To win the battle against your mind, limiting beliefs, and paradigms, start today by creating a first-class war room for your team and yourself.

A war room is a central space for ideas to flourish. If you're working from home, don't put the war room by the TV or in the laundry room. It's too easy to be distracted by that show you wanted to binge on or the shirt you need to iron. Make it a place that encourages creativity.

You can make this a physical or virtual space. Hang up a sign or paper with the team's mission on the wall, that big impossible goal you all are trusting the universe to guide you through. Encourage idea sharing, drawing outside the lines, action plans, and support.

Be sure your personal war room is ready to go, too. That means keeping you in prime operating condition by exercising, eating well, and not drinking the night before. How you do one thing is how you do everything. If there is clutter in your space, whether mental or physical, there's probably clutter in your mind, too.

That clutter keeps you from having the space to have those big, incredible ideas. It's keeping you from dreaming huge and seeing the wide-open possibilities around you.

Clutter can also take the form of fear or a mindset of scarcity. It's like keeping a plant in the dark. It doesn't get the necessary light to grow and achieve all it can be.

> You already have all the resources
> you need in your mind.

In his book *Think and Grow Rich,* Napoleon Hill said that anything could grow if you nurture and feed the soil regularly. However, if you ignore the soil and don't prune out the negative thoughts about fear, failure, or scarcity, they will become weeds and eventually overrun your mental garden.

HOW TO 180 YOUR THINKING

It's your mindset, not your location or your manpower, that is the problem. The paradigm is winning, and the projects you are working on are likely stalling or falling short. Change the paradigm, and you change the future.

How do you combat that mindset issue? The same way we did in Chapter One. By thinking differently.

Play a game with your mind and ask yourself (or your team) these questions:

- What would our company be like if we didn't lack resources?

- How would the business run?

- How would our team feel coming to work every day?

- What successes and pinnacles could we reach?

In your mind, I want you to see the answers to these questions, feel them, and connect with them. When you do that, it shifts your energy from lack to creation. As you go through this mental exercise, examine each area of your company. *What would you be able to do if you changed that segment of your business?*

Then what?

I can hear you asking that because I hear it from my clients. They have the ideal in their mind (which is the majority of the battle), but they still aren't sure how to get from fantasy to reality. To make the dream actually happen.

I have a five-step process I nicknamed COATS that I use with my clients:

1. **Commit**: Make a committed decision that this is the star your company is shooting for. Commit to that big, faraway star, whether it's a million dollars in sales this year or expansion into five states. When you make that committed decision, you are in harmony with your dream and the energy in the universe.

2. **Options**: Write down ten different ways you can get to that star. Is it hiring more people? Expanding your offerings? Concentrating on your profit centers?

3. **Avenues**: Whittle those down to two or three avenues that you can tackle. You have to have a plan, and a plan can't go in too many directions at once.

4. **Targets and Timelines**: Decide as a team what milestones you want to reach and when. For instance, to have a million dollars in sales this year, you need to have a quarter million in sales each quarter and just over $62k each month. Just as there has to be an end goal, there should also be a target deadline. Make it reasonable, but also one that will take effort to achieve.

5. **Step**: You don't have to see every step ahead of you to embark on your plan. Just take that first step, and trust that the Universal Laws already have the next step ready for you.

This method can work for big dreams and little dreams. Maybe you have a couple of tasks in your business that you hate doing, like bookkeeping or sales. Make a list of all the things you hate doing in your job, and then imagine a future with another person right beside you doing those things. Imagine a bookkeeper at the desk or a salesperson making those cold calls. If that person existed, how would your time be better spent? Close your eyes and see yourself going about your day with those hours freed up for other productive tasks.

When we think about the perpetual transmutation of energy that Einstein wrote about, then we realize that our thoughts can also be transmuted into actions and goals. It's not enough to just dream it because it's far too easy for fear and doubt to creep in.

WHAT IS YOUR *DRISHTI*?

Willpower will be the fuel in that first step as you build your belief and trust in the universe. When the belief becomes deep-rooted, it powers all the other steps and makes your confidence in your goal so absolute that anything less seems absurd. The vision becomes your single point of focus, your Drishti in yoga, and then every move you make brings you closer to where you want to be.

Post your goals and KPIs in the war room. Talk about them and reaffirm them to yourself until you believe they will happen. It takes effort to change an old paradigm. When you instill that belief in yourself and your team, it becomes part of the corporate culture. As with the soil, whatever you nurture your company with grows and thrives.

CHAPTER 4

UNDERSTAND MOTIVATION FACTOR

> When you squeeze an orange, orange juice comes out, because that's what's inside. When you are squeezed, what comes out is what is inside.
>
> DR. WAYNE DYER

In my second week of boot camp, the familiar notes of reveille played at some insanely early hour that seemed even earlier than it had the morning before. I groaned and thought, *I don't want to do this*. I didn't want to get up and run five miles, do countless pushups, and practice drills all day. Again. And again. And again.

Boot camp is a lot of repetition of the same difficult things. When I first arrived, I was eager and enthusiastic. I had excelled at many of the things I had attempted in my life, and I was sure I could do that here, too. It's not like I walked into Lackland Air Force Base in Texas completely unprepared—I'd been a runner and athlete for years. It didn't matter. Boot camp is a whole other level of training, no matter who you are. It's tough, exhausting, and designed to break you down before it builds you up again.

I could feel myself getting stronger each day, but as we all gained stamina and muscles, the training instructors piled on the tasks and challenges. I began to lose that enthusiasm I started with, and my motivation dipped. I looked at the tough weeks still ahead of me, and all I wanted to do was go home. I wondered if I'd made the right decision to enlist. The next step seemed impossible, and I couldn't see the way forward.

IS YOUR ENVIRONMENT LYING TO YOU?

That second week, every muscle in my body hurt. My whole body was thoroughly exhausted, and my brain was on overload. The walls seemed higher, the runs longer, and the obstacles bigger than the day before. I couldn't see the end result—the day I would graduate, strong and ready—because I was blinded by what was around me and inside me.

Often, our environment and circumstances lie to us about our level of success. It's like running against the wind. You feel like you aren't making any progress. The idea of quitting becomes more and more tempting as the doubts in your mind whisper louder and louder with each passing second of struggle.

That's when it's time to stop. Look behind you. See where you started and how far you have come since then. When I looked at how much fitter and stronger, both physically and mentally, I had become by that second week, I could remind myself that I was more than capable of the next challenge and the one after that. It wasn't my body that needed convincing of that fact—it was my mind.

Believe, and your belief will create the fact.

WILLIAM JAMES
THE WILL TO BELIEVE, 1896

James's essay, written more than twelve decades ago, has become the basis of dozens of works by motivational speakers in the present day. Essentially, what you believe becomes fact, from both a negative and positive perspective.

If you believe the goal ahead of you is too big, too difficult, or too impossible, it will be. If you believe you have the chops to make it happen—you will. Your mind is a thousand times more powerful than your body, and if you harness that power correctly, you will achieve much more than you ever dreamed.

The biggest lesson I learned in the military wasn't tactical or physical—it was the *spiritual* link between having your thoughts in alignment and excellent performance. When you believe you can do it, you succeed, simple as that. Changing those old patterns, well, that's not as simple.

We get distracted and lose motivation when we focus too much on what's happening in our immediate surroundings. Maybe you're in sales, and after weeks of successful calls, you have several in a row that end in a *no*. Or worse, people aren't even showing up for the call/sales appointment, and your upward trajectory begins to flatten. You start to think things like: *I stink at this. The market sucks. People don't want what I'm selling. I'm not good at sales.*

What if I told you those limiting beliefs were lying? That a few bad sales calls are not evidence that you are in the wrong field—they're evidence that your thoughts are not in alignment with your dreams.

In Chapter Two, we talked about the goal dip. You begin to reach your goal or even achieve it, and suddenly start feeling fear and doubts. You get distracted, your motivation wanes, and you begin to back away from your plan. You may think this isn't working out or you're reaching too high. Any kind of setback fools you into thinking you should retreat to the comfort of the same-old-same-old approaches (that didn't work before, remember?).

THE BELIEF SYSTEM PROBLEM

Your lack of motivation is rooted in your belief systems, which are engaged in a continuous battle. You can believe in your conscious, intellectual mind that you can sell a million dollars in products this year, while your subconscious mind is saying, *no, you can't.* These two belief systems can operate simultaneously and exist at the same time in your mind, like neighbors in a duplex.

The roadblocks you face, whether it's a feeling of being stuck or lacking motivation, are all the negative self-talk and the fear of failure (those familiar paradigms) that nag at you in the background when you are working toward an achievement.

Those paradigms, along with your self-image and limiting beliefs, all conspire against the conscious belief that *I can do it*. Between 96 and 98% of our behavior is habitual, but that habitual behavior is not powered by your conscious mind as much as your thinking and subconscious mind. This means the habits you are developing and operating from stem from those paradigms and fears, derailing everything you attempt to do. It's like trying to drive north with a car that has two flat tires on one side, forcing the car to veer to the right and go east.

If you want to create different results and remove that block, you have to get your thoughts in alignment. This process is called Praxis, a way of turning a theory into a fact via action and reflection. In other words, retraining your brain, as physical therapists do with stroke victims that are paralyzed on one side.

Your goal is to align your conscious thoughts with your subconscious thoughts and then move that toward the thing you want to be, do, or have. If you don't align these two warring parts of your mind, you're always going to do this kind of one step forward, two steps back dance. We'll get into more specifics of how to do this in the next section of the book. But for now, I just want you to stop and think for a second about these questions:

1. Are your goals coming from a place of lack? A need to prove your worth?

2. Are your goals rooted in a place of joy? A need to create something more and different?

Most of us create goals based on need—money, possessions, status. There is nothing wrong with wanting, desiring, and creating those things. Lack of satisfaction breeds creativity and desire for bigger and better goals simply because we, as humans, are goal-seeking organisms. That isn't coming from lack; it's coming from expansion.

However, too often, we feel like we don't have enough *whatever*, and we kill ourselves trying to build up enough. The problem is there's never enough. You'll always feel that sense of lack, and your subconscious will keep trying to protect you from possible failure by draining your motivation unless you realign your thinking.

WORK WITH THE LAW OF COMPENSATION

The Law of Compensation, which is based on Ralph Waldo Emerson's essay, "Compensation," comprises three concepts: the need for what you do, your ability to do it, and the difficulty of replacing you. Concentrate on the first two, and the third will naturally happen. You will see that generous compensation because you have created a need for yourself and your skills. Most of us focus too much on the compensation end instead of being the best at what we do.

We also worry that we aren't making progress fast enough or aren't working hard enough, and that's why we haven't achieved those financial goals. We get so mired in the weeds we can't see the flowers sprouting at the edge of the field. We want to see results right away, when that isn't how things work. You wouldn't plant a bunch of carrot seeds and dig them up every day to see if they are taking root, would you? You have to do the same with your dreams and goals. Trust that the universe has got it, that the seeds you are planting will flourish, and keep moving forward.

I had a client who was experiencing writer's block. In one of our coaching conversations, we talked about her meditation practice and adding morning meditations that would leave her starting her day in a refreshed, peaceful, and relaxed state. Creativity comes from a relaxed state when you allow the brain to have room to think and dream big.

KNOW THE HABITS THAT ARE DRAGGING YOU DOWN

If you want new results, you have to create new habits that work for you, not against you.

Be a Leader: Spend an hour a day reading an article or book that increases your knowledge base. To develop as a leader, you need to enrich your personal soil and focus on being the best.

Celebrate the Wins: We can become demotivated when we let circumstances serve as evidence that we aren't doing well. Did somebody say no in your last two sales calls? Celebrate the fact that you are making the calls. Then focus on perfecting your presentation by learning more about your field.

Use Your Energy: When we face a setback, many of us withdraw and conserve our energy. I know how tempting that can be. We feel like wounded animals; all we want to do is stay in the den and avoid the world. It's that fight-or-flight response triggered by the amygdala. Remember: Energy is endless. Don't let yourself sit idle and waste this valuable resource.

Give to Get: When you are feeling unmotivated, go out and serve others. Ask yourself, *how can I give my current client base more today?* That shifts the focus off of you and your problems and gives you a new way of moving forward. It's like being on a long and difficult run with another person who is struggling. When you focus on encouraging them to take the next step or climb the next hill, you forget how hard the run is because you are too busy lifting up the person beside you.

It's Not about the Goal: It's not reaching the goal that's most important—it's expanding who you are as a human being. A goal is merely part of the progressive realization of a worthy ideal. We are goal-seeking organisms, but when we focus only on that singular win, we lose sight of the bigger picture.

Remain in a Place of Gratitude: Being continuously grateful keeps your energy high and your enthusiasm strong.

Don't Discount Dissatisfaction: Because humans need and want goals, we also experience dissatisfaction with the status quo. You can use that as fuel to dream bigger. The Wright Brothers, for example, were bicycle mechanics who dreamed of flying. It seemed like an impossible dream, but the Wright Brothers knew they could develop a faster way of getting from A to B. They used that dissatisfaction to propel their idea into a reality.

Nothing is All Good (Or All Bad): The Law of Polarity says that all spectrums have opposite ends, both good and bad, like the North and South Poles. However, nothing is 100% north or south, and if you look for the good instead of the bad, you will tip those scales in a more positive direction.

I've been where you are. When I started transitioning away from my full-time job and into coaching, my initial goal was to replace the six figures I was already earning. As I began to leave the safety net of my job, I looked at the sheer volume of calls, networking, and sales I would have to make to maintain my income. When I figured out the sell-through percentages, I was overwhelmed. I'd need to make X number of calls to have Y success rate. My days got longer, and I had to use my weekends to catch up. Before I knew it, I was stuck in the very rat race I was trying to escape, feeling more and more resentment every day.

I sat down with Bob Proctor and told him how overwhelmed, stressed, and frustrated I was feeling. He said, "I only want you to talk to two people a week. No more. If you can't move one of them to work with you, then step back and work on your presentation."

Two people? Instead of twenty or thirty? Immediately, I felt relief, but then I also began to panic. How was I going to maintain my sales on *two* calls a week?

It seemed counterintuitive, but I trusted Bob and decided that if he told me to stand on my head and sing the alphabet, I would do it. So I cut down to two calls a week and worked on my presentation. Almost immediately, I began to love my business again, and that joy showed in everything I did, which drew people to my positive energy. I was able to very quickly quadruple my income and became the top 1% of coaches for Bob Proctor.

This, I realized, was the effortless way to success. The path of least resistance. All that grit and grind hadn't moved me into success as well as gratitude and joy did. I was aligning with my own source of energy—and it was working.

Whether you believe energy comes from a higher power or from science and Einstein, the fact is energy is always there and working with you. If you allow the naysayers, social media, competitors, or your own paradigms to diffuse that energy, you will be forever mired. Redirect that energy intelligently, and use your mind to draw you closer to success. Dig up the carrots or trust that all your nurturing will make them grow. It's your choice.

PART TWO

THE SOLUTIONS

CHAPTER 5

REALIGN YOUR VIEWPOINT

By this point in the book, you should have a handle on what the problems are with your business. However, changing the way you do things isn't as easy as just snapping your fingers. Even though a lot of what I talk about in this book centers on your thoughts, you'd be surprised at how tough it is to corral your thoughts in more constructive and imaginative directions.

The biggest obstacle my clients face in changing how they do things is believing it can happen and holding onto that positive belief. They can dream the impossible goal and imagine the life they will lead or the things they will do, but as soon as they stop dreaming, reality steps in, and they go back to hearing all the *can'ts* and *shouldn'ts* and *won'ts* in their mind. Their thoughts are filled with all those huge roadblocks and massive mountains they have to scale to reach that dream.

Our analytical mind is a gift; it really is. It helps us do a thousand different things during the day—except for dreaming. Too often, we become servants of our analytical minds, believing all the *can'ts* thrown our way instead of going deeper and listening to our hearts. When you serve your heart and soul, you are working from a place of truth. Then you are in control of your mind, versus your mind being in control of you.

PERMISSION TO DREAM

I had a client who had a great job at a TV station and had won several accolades. She'd achieved everything she set out to do, yet she was still feeling a sense of dissatisfaction, that "is this all there is?" feeling that so many of us have. We had a conversation about what other job she might have or what else she could do with her life, and for a long time, she was stymied. Then I told her to simply give herself permission to dream.

Adults sometimes think it's silly to dream—but that's just the analytical mind talking. The only way to get to your heart's desires is to take the time to *hear* your heart. When my client started to dream, she realized she loved to travel and loved social media. She decided to leave her job, start a social media company, and travel the world. Within three months, she was earning six figures and hiring more staff. The manifestation of her dream happened quickly because she shook off the shackles of her analytical brain and decided she would only serve her heart's desires.

Sounds crazy, right? Give yourself permission to do the illogical, and the illogical can happen.

Your paradigms—those inner beliefs you have developed since birth that dictate what you think can/will happen—don't just change how you see the world; they also control how you set goals, even what you give yourself permission to think about and dream. Have you ever been at work and started to imagine yourself flying to the moon? Then you stop yourself, thinking that's not a realistic dream because an ordinary person can never get to space. Well, Jeff Bezos and Richard Branson would disagree. They let go of those paradigms and achieved something amazing.

As far as we know, we are the only creatures on this planet that fantasize. Achieving those dream goals is all about taking your fantasy and turning it into a theory and then a reality. Bob Proctor talks about Sir Edmund

Hillary, the first person to climb Mt. Everest. No one had ever done that before, and people thought he was crazy. Anyone who had been on that mountain had died.

Hillary had dreamed of climbing Mt. Everest for years. When he thought about doing it, he asked himself two questions:

1. Am I willing to pay the price, whatever that is?
2. Am I able?

People do the impossible every single day (as Hillary did). Think about the Wright Brothers, Elon Musk, Steve Jobs, et al. There are hundreds—no, thousands of people who have taken the power that flows through all of us and used that to accomplish the impossible. If you think about that power, which we use a fraction of over the course of our lifetimes, then the answer to *Am I able?* is yes. The ability is there; it just needs you to believe in it.

> God's gift to you is more talent and ability than you could possibly use in your lifetime. Your gift to God is to develop as much of that talent and ability as you can in this lifetime.
>
> STEVE BOW

THE ABCS OF GOALS

There are three types of goals (and we are going to get into this in more depth in the next chapter):

"A" Goals: These are things you know you can do. For instance, maybe you want to run a marathon. But you ran one four years ago, so you already know you can do it. There isn't any growth attached to an A goal. Reaching for these kinds of goals over and over again can leave you bored and resentful.

"B" Goals: These are the goals you *think* you can do. For instance, if your company grossed a million dollars last year, and your B goal is to increase that amount by 10% next quarter, that's probably a doable goal. You already know how to earn a million dollars; you're just earning a bit more. That's not growth. You're still moving laterally.

"C" Goals: These goals are completely based on our wants and desires. They're not a little stretch—they're a huge stretch. If you can close your eyes and plan how you'll get to your C goal right now, then it's not a big enough goal. When a goal isn't big enough, you can get bored and eventually give up because you're not inspired.

That was me several years ago. I was doing the marathons, competing in triathlons, the half Ironmans, and accumulating degrees. I was achieving A and B goals and was caught in the rat race. I was miserable until I imagined a C goal.

It was an impossible goal. Something crazy, too big, something I couldn't even begin to figure out how to accomplish. My C goal was to make enough money to fund three villages in Africa and fund three college educations for kids who couldn't afford college. And it's happening. I've funded one and a half villages, and I raised $220,000 for the tuition. I'll be watching not just three kids but twenty kids graduate in 2023. If I had stayed in the rat race, I never would have been able to have that kind of impact. I would have kept going through the same maze every single day, never escaping and hitting my true potential.

> The rat race is a killer, literally. Realize that you are not your job. You are not your role in the office. You are a spirit in a body, and you have a purpose for being here. We are so much greater than a job.

If we accept that we are bigger than the time clock we punch, then we can start asking ourselves: *If I garner this much success, how do I serve, and how do I inspire others?* For me, that was how the idea of the villages came into being. I'm working to inspire others to make an impact and leave a legacy not only for them but for their communities and the world.

YOU DON'T NEED A MONEY PLAN

When I tell people they don't need a plan for how they will have the money to achieve their dream, they think I'm crazy. *What do you mean, I don't need to figure out where the money is coming from?*

I mean exactly that. When you start worrying about the how and why of achieving your dream, you start letting the analytical mind take over. Before you know it, all the roadblocks and obstacles will loom over you again.

> The Law of Compensation says that we will be compensated in direct comparison to the need for what we do and the difficulty in replacing us. If you are making something or offering a service that people need, a thing that only you can do, you will be compensated.

What you do need is a plan for the money *after* you earn it. What will reaching this goal mean, and what will you do with that success? Are you going to cultivate more relationships? Help others? Build a legacy? Most people are so caught up in the day-to-day of the rat race that they don't have the bandwidth to even consider their legacy.

When I dreamed of helping those villages in Africa and sending kids to college, that dream was close to my heart. I was emotionally connected to achieving that, which gave me clarity and the impetus to change my behavior.

As we mentioned earlier, the key is creating an emotional connection to your goal so that you are so inspired you naturally change your behavior. That's how we grow as a human race.

KEEPING THE FOCUS

I've known people who were really excited and so strongly connected with their goal that it made them cry. But they didn't connect those goals with actions because they couldn't see the path of steps ahead. You don't have to see all the steps—only the first one.

Sometimes you can feel a painful distant wish instead of a joyful desire. That stems from a lack mentality, which traps you in negative thinking that pushes your goal away instead of drawing it to you.

To change that paradigm, remind yourself every day what you want and what that means to your heart. You can put your goal on a vision board or state it daily with affirmations. However, both of those things are just tools. They don't do anything on their own. You have to live with that goal in your mind and release all the worries and stress.

Then you will be able to take inspired action every day. Those aren't just regular actions—they're actions inspired by your goal, your dream, and your heart.

When you are constantly connecting with your goal, it helps you make the right choice with any decision or crossroads. If an idea comes to you, even if it doesn't make sense (like starting a podcast or writing a movie), you get quiet and listen to your heart. Does it echo with you emotionally? Don't let your analytical mind stop you from taking that next step.

Those inspired action steps are your internal GPS, aligning you with getting to where you have dreamed of being. When you stop holding onto that dream, all the fear, worry, and doubt creep in and you freeze, caught in the hows and whats. Just like your car, no amount of GPS will direct you if you stop moving.

TRUST IN THE UNIVERSE

When you step out on a bridge, you trust that the girders and deck will hold you. You walk across it without ever worrying that the bridge is just going to disappear. The problem is that people have a much easier time trusting the tangible bridge than the intangible universe.

You have a choice—you can either fear or have faith. When you are afraid, you don't act, or you act in negative ways. When you have faith, you trust that this will happen and release the anxiety about it.

The reticular activating system in your brain is trained to find more of what you feed it. If you focus on the negatives, your brain will only see more of that and find evidence to support your negative theory. It also works the opposite—if you focus on the positives and the joy in your dream, your brain will see all the pluses and none of the roadblocks.

No matter what you focus on, you will always find evidence to support that viewpoint. What are you going to choose to focus on today?

The Law of Attraction works the same way. When you have positive energy, you start attracting the people, events, and moments that respond to that energy. When your energy is poor, people can sense that. As the old saying goes, you can't paint a turd. Underneath, it's still a turd, and people will know. If you feel desperation or anxiety, you will attract more things to worry about and repel people who sense that desperation.

I remember Sandy Gallagher, who worked with Bob Proctor, telling me a story that really resonated with me. She dreamed of having a house on the beach. She kept focusing on it and focusing on it and found exactly that, a house on the beach for the amount of money she wanted to pay. Then she realized that living on the beach meant waves crashing on her property and cleaning salt off the windows, so she needed to get more specific about her dream.

She bought a second house, but it wasn't quite the one she dreamed of. Then she saw a third house that was exactly what she had envisioned, right down to the last detail. However, it was way out of her price range. Bob Proctor told her to go visit the house. "Tell the Realtor to leave you alone in the house. Then I want you to visualize yourself in that house with your family, having Christmas dinner," he said.

She trusted him and did exactly that. She put an offer in even though she didn't have the money. She went a step further and sent letters to her family, inviting them for Christmas dinner at a house she didn't own yet. She trusted the universe would make it happen and kept taking inspired actions in that direction.

Then she found some money she didn't know she had, and all the pieces of the financing slipped into place. She moved into that house and invited her family over for Christmas dinner and lived the dream she had had for so long.

Whatever you want, it's up to you to change the way you think. You can either get there kicking and screaming or with ease and flow, strolling through doors that are a yes everywhere you turn. Don't allow those negative thoughts in your head to manifest. Instead, nurture the positive beliefs until they are the only words you hear.

CHAPTER 6

SET FAR-OUT GOALS

Each person is born with an infinite power, against which no earthly force is of the slightest significance.

NEVILLE GODDARD

That Goddard quote is the basis of everything you need to do and believe before you can set those huge, scary, far-out goals. I bet a large number of you reading this book have already thought of a dozen external circumstances that will stop you from achieving your goals. You're not smart enough, tall enough, wealthy enough, whatever enough to reach your pinnacle.

That's simply not true. When you believe those things, you are placing power in external circumstances and yanking the power away from yourself. It's like planning a trip to California and then giving your car to someone else and hoping they'll give you a ride.

The first thing you have to understand and truly believe is that there is a power that already resides deep inside you, whether that power is spirit, source, the universe, or God. Let me say that again:

> You have to truly believe there
> is already a power inside you
> to make these goals happen.

Read that sentence again and again until you start to feel it in your bones. If you allow external circumstances, doubts, or fears to hold you back, you'll be back in that car with a stranger who is taking you to Minnesota instead of San Diego and running on fumes.

Truly knowing you have that power inside you is a *choice multiplier*. It's freedom, true freedom with a limitless future. When we rely solely on our brains to achieve impossible things, it stunts our growth, joy, fulfillment, and success. People like Steve Jobs, the Wright Brothers, Albert Einstein, and Thomas Edison didn't listen to the naysayers. They didn't believe their doubts. They didn't take stock of the reasons why their ideas shouldn't work. They simply believed with every fiber of their being that their goals could happen.

> Within the macro view of the world lies your true potential. Being stuck in the micro view, where you are worrying about every little detail, is being in survival mode. You're stuck on that hamster wheel and struggling to find a way off. You're coming at everything from a mechanical viewpoint instead of a spiritual belief system.

Don't let the analytical mind lead you; it's a poor master. If you are feeling frustrated, unfulfilled, or stuck in a continuous loop, chances are you are letting your mind lead you instead of your heart. You can promise to do better all day long, but if you don't shift your paradigms and dare to think in a new way, nothing will change.

START WITH THE VISION

Everything in this world is created twice—once in our minds, and then once in physical form. The people who allowed their energy and spirit to take the wheel dared to dream the impossible and then make it true. They had a vision, no idea of how they would get there, and an innate, unwavering belief that it would happen. Then they saw it manifest in the physical world.

FIND **BEST** BELIEVING FRIENDS

Great friends will tell you what to do, and caution you, because that's what great friends are supposed to do. Best friends, however, don't do that because they know there are plans for you that you cannot see. Best friends simply say, *Go for it.*

We don't want to start with A or B goals; we want to go right for those C goals. Smart, measurable, attainable—those are all adjectives we don't want to use. Impossible, huge, unlimited—that's how you should be thinking.

"Change your conception of yourself and you will automatically change the world in which you live" is another of my favorite Goddard quotes. Think of yourself as having limitless potential. Dare to think of yourself as great and capable of *anything*.

PUT A PRIORITY ON THINKING

This might sound crazy, but I want you to give yourself permission to simply think. We spend so much time in our lives being busy. We don't spend anywhere near enough time dreaming and manifesting.

First thing in the morning, or at the end of the day, when you're a little tired (because your mind won't resist these big thoughts when you're tired), refrain from checking emails, answering calls, or logging into social media. Put yourself first and go to a place where you won't be disturbed. For the next thirty minutes, I want you to just think.

Yes, thirty minutes. Give your brain time to expand, dream, and imagine. Allow the ideas to just free flow. Write them on a pad of paper without judging them or worrying about the "how." If you're a controller like me, you will have a strong urge to figure out how on earth you will get there. Don't do that. Simply write it down.

If you come up with a goal and already know how to achieve it, that's not a C goal. It's not worthy of you and the power inside you. Dream bigger.

Let your mind wander: What lifestyle do you want? What workflow would you like to have? What's the ideal team surrounding you? What is their attitude? How do you direct them? Do you take time off during the day to walk in nature or meet up with a friend for coffee? How often do you want to work? Four days a week? Three weeks a month? At the end of the day, are you really making a difference in your work? Are you being handsomely compensated, and as a result, you can give to the causes that are important to you? Whatever these answers are, write them down.

After a couple of weeks of doing this exercise, you will start to notice themes among the things you have written down. Now you can start narrowing the list. Choose the one thing that excites you and scares you at the same time. The thing that makes you feel emotional or shed tears of joy. If that happens, you know you're going in the right direction.

I'm not talking about a painful want. That kind of feeling comes from a place of lack. Instead, feel a *joyful desire* for this far-out goal. When you feel joyful desire, you are putting yourself in harmony with what the universe sees for you.

Now make a committed decision that, come hell or high water, you are making this happen.

FOCUS ON THE WHAT, NOT THE HOW

When I was in the military, I commuted and worked twelve-hour days. I knew I wanted to go into business for myself, but the thought of finding the time to talk to fifty potential clients per week seemed insurmountable. I did it anyway and was quickly hit with burnout.

Bob Proctor sat me down, told me to connect with my vision for my lifestyle, and told me to rethink how I was growing my business. His advice worked because I stopped operating from a point of exhausted desperation; I was fueled by my vision.

> When you focus on the *what* instead of the *how*, the universe has your back. It will use your mental faculties to capitalize on the right opportunities to move faster and further instead of wasting valuable mental energy on the grit and grind.

In *The Dore Lectures on Mental Science,* Thomas Troward discusses the connection between science and spirit: ". . . in a word, we find ourselves brought face to face with a power which exhibits on a stupendous scale, the faculties of selection and adaption of means to ends, and thus distributes energy and life in accordance with a recognizable scheme of cosmic progression." In essence, if you start with spirit, the mechanical falls into place.

The people who have made the greatest advances in physical science have clearly seen the subordination of the mechanism to the spiritual. The Wright Brothers believed they could find a way to make man fly, even though we didn't have wings or technology that could make that happen. When you allow the mechanical to limit you, it keeps you from rising to your highest form.

When I work with clients, I teach them how to tap into their imagination and intuition. We use this technique with CEOs, teams, and with individuals. I tell them that when we dream big, we can make big things happen. Allowing your mind to expand and reach for impossible things makes room for that first step to manifest in your thoughts. Take that first step, and the next one will show itself, and so on.

Many coaches will tell you to wait to make these plans until after you have clients and a business in place or to achieve A before going after B (and don't even think about achieving Z yet). If you do that, you are limiting yourself.

Allow yourself to imagine the possibilities before the beginning is even built.

Novak Djokovic, who won three major tennis titles in 2021 after a meteoric career, has said many times that he dreamed of winning Wimbledon long before he even reached the grass courts. "I think when I was six or seven years old, I was making this improvised Wimbledon trophy and imagining, looking myself in the mirror, and lifting that trophy, and imagining I'll be standing one day on Centre Court." That impossible dream happened for him, even though all the odds were against him.

BE PREPARED FOR A BATTLE

The more you prepare for what's to come, the more your old paradigms will fight you. Those paradigms want you to stay in your comfort zone. They will whisper doubts and negative self-talk. When you open that door by allowing those doubts to take over your mind, those old paradigms just waltz in and try to take over. I suggest keeping a journal to write down all these counterthoughts. Then you will be able to see some of the outdated beliefs that are holding you back.

Your paradigms will want you to look outside yourself for the answers you want (and remember, those external things are the very limits holding you back). When I was caught in the rat race, I was climbing all these mountains because I thought this mountain would make me happy or that one would. None of them did because I was looking *outside* myself for answers and fulfillment when that secret sauce was already inside me.

Look to the people who inspire you when you are struggling. What would they do? How would they act? Those people, who have achieved their far-out goals, are giving you clues on how to shift your thinking.

One of my clients had received several great job offers but ultimately declined all of them. I asked her why. All of the job offers seemed to fit her wants and needs, but I knew that her choice to decline some great offers was an indication that the jobs weren't fitting with what she truly, deep down inside, wanted. We talked through the different offers, and as we did, she gained clarity on what was going on in her heart. One job had everything she wanted, but it was an office job with a terrible commute. I asked her, "What's the opposite of that?"

She thought for a second. "I really want flexibility in my schedule and the ability to travel."

We talked about the next job she turned down, one that had the flexibility she wanted but didn't have the culture she was seeking. "I'd rather be around upbeat, enthusiastic people," she told me.

Those discussions gave her the clarity she needed to find a job with a great environment, flexible hours, some travel, and no commute. She didn't just thrive in that new position; she became a rockstar at the company because she was so happy. She was working from what her spirit told her, not the mechanics of what a job should be. You don't have to be an entrepreneur to have everything you want. Even a "regular" job can give you total flexibility with your schedule or give you one week off a month. Be clear about what you truly want and have the courage to ask for it.

As you start writing things down when you brainstorm your goals, you'll be creating a shopping list for the life you want. When your belief system starts popping up and saying, "That's not for you," or "You shouldn't go after that," I want you to question where those beliefs came from. Were they passed down to you? Did you cultivate them out of fear? Then ask yourself:

> What would be different in my life if I stopped listening to those false beliefs?

To move forward instead of laterally, you will need to do some mental housekeeping to remove those old paradigms that don't serve you and hold you back. You will grow. You will change. That's exactly what a C goal should make you do.

When you want a team to dream really big, bring them together regularly to relax, brainstorm, fantasize, and create a shopping list of the team's wants and dreams. Narrow the list down to one main goal, and ask the team how motivated they are to work toward that goal. If they tell you it's something they think they *should* do rather than something they want to do, it's not the right goal.

MAINTAIN YOUR FOCUS

Once you have decided on your far-out goal, write it down on a card or piece of paper and keep it with you at all times. Dream about it. Think about it. Talk about it. Get emotionally involved with your goal. Start imagining how things would change if you achieved that goal. Keep a running list of action steps you can take toward that goal, but open your mind to other possible paths that the universe will bring you. Use those nudges to spur inspired actions.

When you do that, you start living from the goal, which changes your paradigms, changes your behavior, and ultimately changes your life.

The most important component, and probably the number-one thing to take away from this book, is the importance of the decision. You have to *decide* to let go of those old paradigms. Decide to stop listening to naysayers. Decide to dream big and go for it. Bob Proctor has a great article on deciding[4] that inspired me so much that I read it three times and cried when I realized the power of who I can be and who I am meant to be.

Decide today to set a far-out goal. Decide today to believe that goal is possible. Decide today to stop being weighed down by the *buts* and the *hows*. Once you make that decision, the universe will gladly light the path ahead of your feet.

4   https://www.proctorgallagherinstitute.com/tips-and-tools/ decision-making

CHAPTER 7

BUILD
THE MISSION

Rather than being an onlooker thinking of the end, become a partaker, thinking from the end.

NEVILLE GODDARD

In previous chapters, we talked about setting your goals, writing them down, and keeping them uppermost in your mind. Now, we will talk about how we begin getting to that goal.

I highly recommend reading the Desire chapter in *Think and Grow Rich* by Napoleon Hill. That talks about how you fix the idea in your head, establish what your intentions are, set a date for achieving your wants, then put a plan in place, and create a clear and concise statement of what you are striving for so you can read it aloud twice daily and keep your mind fixed on the goal. Write the statement in the present tense as if you are already there. Read it once in the morning and once before going to bed. Every time you read that statement, see and feel yourself in possession of your goal.

THE 3-3-3 EXERCISE

To create your action plan, you have to begin brainstorming. For that, I like to reference the 3-3-3 exercise, which is used to train your mind to see and find solutions. It's based on a story about a man who owned a radio station in Canada. A tornado hit one of the towns, devastating the population. He wanted to help his community, so he brought together several town leaders and asked them, "Do you want to raise three million dollars in three hours and get it funded in three days?"

People thought he was crazy. "How do you think that will happen?" someone asked him.

He replied, "I didn't ask you how you think it will happen; I asked do you want to do it." He went up to a whiteboard and created two columns. On the left, he wrote *Why We Can't*. On the right, he wrote, *How We Can.* He drew a giant X through the left side. "We're only going to brainstorm how we can. No ideas are bad ideas. If anyone comes up with a reason it can't be done or an obstacle, we all have permission to say 'next' and move on to the next idea."

One person said, "All the radio stations can come together and raise money." Another replied, "But all the radio stations are in competition. They won't do that." The man said, "next!"

"We can get a celeb to emcee the fundraising show," someone suggested. Another person said it would be impossible to get a celebrity to work for free on short notice. "Next!" the man said, and they moved on to another idea.

The town leaders brainstormed ways to accomplish those goals that others tried to naysay. As a result, all of the radio stations rallied together in a short amount of time. They brought in a celebrity to headline the fundraiser, raised three million dollars in three hours, and had that money funded within three days.

The 3-3-3 Exercise allows you to be creative and toss out all kinds of ideas and strategies. Remember, this is a C goal, one that seems so "out there" you have no idea how to get there. Just close your eyes, picture yourself in that space, in possession of that goal, and start brainstorming. Nothing is off-limits. If your brain tries to shoot it down, say "next!" and move on. If your idea is to jump off the moon and land on a pile of soft puppies, that's great. Jot it down and keep thinking.

> If you say *"next!"* every time you need to know the answers or how it can be done, you are training your mind to stay open to all possibilities. Do this for a few minutes every day. Before you know it, you'll be learning how to play a mind game that encourages expansive thinking. You can brainstorm with other people, or use this exercise in your mastermind group.

NARROW DOWN TO TWO

Once you have your list of strategies, cross off the ideas that are truly crazy (maybe the jumping off the moon one is a bit too farfetched). Then pick two strategies to begin working on. I want you to write a description of the strategy and what it will take. Beneath that, list the steps needed to execute the strategy and then organize those action items in terms of importance. You've just created a to-do list for your goal.

> Those two factors: a clear, concise statement of the goal, and a timeline for achieving it, are the ingredients for success.

As you write up your plan, list any specialized knowledge you need to acquire to achieve your goal. Maybe it's understanding the stock market or speaking French. Whatever those specialties are, don't concern yourself with where those skills will come from. You might not have to learn that skill set at all. When you allow the ideas to exist without stifling them, you're leveraging the power of the mind. Those Universal Laws are already working to bring you the necessary talents for yourself or other people.

Maybe you need specific people with skills and resources, like a lawyer or CPA. Write a name down for those resources. If you don't know a person, start looking for someone with the specialized knowledge you need to achieve that goal.

BUILD A MASTERMIND GROUP FOR SUPPORT

The first place to start for specialized knowledge is your team of support. Choose people who have some of the knowledge and experience that you need to implement your goal and who have positive attitudes. They can be inside or outside your organization. What is most important is that they possess knowledge, effort, and a spirit of harmony for the attainment of a purpose.

Don't be afraid to be choosy. This is your future you're talking about, and you want people who will help you get there, not hold you back. Once you determine the key players of your mastermind group, you can begin leveraging the power of their collective thinking, just as the man did in the 3-3-3 Exercise.

Price Pritchett has a book called *You Squared*, in which he talks about the things you need to do that take you beyond the next step. Incremental steps don't get you there because you're only taking baby steps and disrupting the flow that can be found in taking big leaps.

That's why your mastermind group is so important. If you start talking about making huge moves and they tell you that's outrageous, ridiculous, or crazy, they're not going to help you advance. Remember, the masses are controlled by paradigms, and the more you stay stuck within those, the harder it is to go after those big goals. Achievers only choose paradigms that are in harmony with their goals, and they are forever breaking them and creating new paradigms as their goals shift.

BUILD AN EFFECTIVE MASTERMIND GROUP

As you did with goal-setting, don't be afraid to reach out to those leaders you admire as you build your mastermind group. You want to be surrounded by people who challenge you, lift you up, and encourage you to stretch your boundaries and thinking.

Masterminding requires an open mind and a release of any crippling beliefs. The more you work with the mastermind, the more powerful it becomes and the more answers you will find in your group. Results are much easier to accomplish when you have a whole group of people cheering you along and helping you think of those big ideas.

Napoleon Hill, in *Think and Grow Rich*, offers a fabulous guideline for leading a successful mastermind group. In addition, he clearly defines the group as *the coordination of knowledge and effort between two or more people who work towards a definite purpose in a spirit of harmony . . . no two minds ever come together without thereby creating a third, invisible, intangible force, which may be likened to a third mind.*

The person leading the meeting should have a copy of this definition and the guidelines, and share them with the group. When we connect with those principles, it reminds us that we are there to serve others.

There are no hard and fast rules. You can meet weekly or whenever someone has a problem. You can have five people, or you can have seven. I don't recommend having a huge mastermind group because it's hard for everyone to get time to be heard.

Be sure to have order in the meeting and a timekeeper. Honor your commitment to the group and show up for every meeting. Start on time, finish on time, and be respectful of the time when you have the floor. Each person should have a couple of minutes to share a win since the last meeting and then a few minutes to talk about their "ask" from the group for that week.

You might have to teach people to get to the point, but it will be worth it. If the group is ineffective because someone is rambling or because people aren't consistent about attending, it will dissolve.

When someone has an ask, everyone in the mastermind group can popcorn answers (like in the 3-3-3 Exercise). As the asker, you don't dismiss their suggestions. You listen, write them down, and later follow through on what they offered for ideas. If you're the type of person to say this won't work before you even try it, you will not be successful in a mastermind group.

As the group celebrates wins, it's a good time to discuss some of the steps and leaps the achievers took because that can breed a culture of risk-taking. Keep all discussions focused and deliberate. People want to be nice and socialize, but that shouldn't happen during the meeting.

The purpose of the mastermind is to solve problems and find solutions—that's it. It's not a garden club or a reunion. If it feels like you're lollygagging, you won't be committed to the group and will leave because your time is valuable. Keeping the conversations on track builds that level of trust with the other people in the group.

MAKE A DAILY COMMITMENT TO ACTION

Once you have your ideas for strategies from your 3-3-3 Exercise and your mastermind group, you have to commit every day to take inspired action.

That means taking some quiet time in the morning and living inside your goal in your mind. Then create a running list of at least six action steps to take toward the goal. I'm not talking about busywork like organizing the filing cabinet. I'm talking about inspired action steps that force you to reach higher and further than ever before.

Make a time commitment by blocking off time on your calendar for lead-generating activities, goal-achieving habits, prospect meetings, events, or simply quiet thinking time. If you don't put these things on your calendar, they won't happen. Most of us bend over backward to serve the organization we work for and leave the scraps of time for our goals. I'm asking you to flip this approach and plot *your* thinking time first. You'll quickly find that you are more effective in less time and that every step you take toward your goal is more impactful and further-reaching. It becomes a leap, not just a baby step.

CHAPTER 8
CREATE
MENTAL KEVLAR

You're clear on your vision, everyone is behind you, and you're moving forward, tackling one inspired action after another. When you set a goal that is worthy of you and your gifts, you become inspired to take the path to get there. For a long time, you are motivated and working hard, and then . . .

Nothing. Your enthusiasm begins to wane. You feel defeated because nothing is happening, or things aren't happening as quickly as you want them to. You're tempted to give up, succumb to the old paradigms, and slip back into your familiar habits.

For the record, this happens to everyone. I had a client last week who has been moving her business in a new direction, doing speaking engagements and has been experiencing some success in that area. She had a friend in a similar field who said, "Don't do that now; it's not the right time. Companies aren't spending money because of the pandemic. The funding isn't there."

My client had the confidence to shut down that conversation before her friend's negative thinking permeated her own thinking. She could feel her body tighten up when her friend was saying all those negative things, and she changed the conversation instead of giving it space in her mind, then used her mental faculties to reframe what she had just heard.

There are six mental faculties you can rely upon and use as a point of support, as opposed to relying on other people to prop you up when things get tough. Why not rely on your friends and family? Because they may not be in the right frame of mind to advise you, they may be letting their old paradigms win, and they very likely don't understand what you are doing. If you aren't talking to someone who is very successful at what you are doing, don't ask them for advice. You wouldn't ask a broke person for advice on investing, right? So be selective about who you share your message and vision with.

THE SIX MENTAL FACULTIES FOR SUCCESS

Imagination
Will
Perception
Intuition
Memory
Reason

Once you build your mental Kevlar, you can share your message and vision anywhere; heck, you can shout it from the rooftops. But first, build that strength you need.

MENTAL FACULTY ONE: IMAGINATION

When we are little kids, we're all encouraged to use our imaginations (maybe just to get us out from under our parents' feet). We see adventures in the trees in the backyard, picture a pirate ship in a discarded box, and envision magic animals darting through the forest. As we get older, we're taught that imagination is daydreaming, and that's a negative thing. It's not.

Use the "War Room" you created as a place to let your imagination expand and soar. Give your mind room and space to think and dream big.

Imagination is one of your superpowers. Using your imagination aligns you with solutions instead of problems. I know that because my imagination brought about a huge change in my life.

If you don't believe in the power of imagination, try this exercise. Picture a lemon on your countertop. See the bright yellow of its skin, the dimples, the thickness. Feel the texture of it. Imagine cutting it in half and smelling the tart, citrusy scent. Picture yourself squeezing it and feeling the juice dripping down your palm. Now imagine taking a bite of that lemon—what's happening in your body right now? Are you feeling the anticipation because you love lemons, or are your lips pinched together because you dislike the tartness? Either way, you are feeling that lemon in your body. That's how powerful your mind and imagination are, and your body, remember, is an instrument of your mind.

Several years ago, I had put in my retirement from the military, so I could make this business a full-time venture. My husband decided to do the same, but he got one more assignment in the middle of the country. We were living in Hawaii at the time, a very expensive state and even more expensive on essentially one income and one housing allowance. My business was growing, but it was new, and I couldn't see a way to uproot all of it for a year-long relocation. I started panicking. On the back of an envelope, I scratched out four different financial scenarios, each more dire than before. We couldn't afford to maintain two houses and didn't want to be apart. Then two of my clients' credit cards declined, and I went into a full tailspin of panic about money.

I could feel that anxiety and fear in my gut and the tension in my back. I had to physically stop, then tell myself, "Shut up. Visualize what you *do* want because this isn't helping." Stopping myself at the moment cut off the spiral of panic and helped me redirect myself until I felt ease and flow. I settled into the surety that everything would work out, my husband and I wouldn't be separated, and we would move on to the next phase.

The next day, two clients called and asked if they could pay the balance of their monthly coaching fees in full. A few days after that, my husband's assignment was canceled for no real reason we could ever figure out.

It just happened. I had imagined that things would all work out, that we would continue to live where we did, and that money would flow to my company. I imagined—and I believed.

MENTAL FACULTY TWO: WILL

You can literally will things into existence if you believe hard enough, don't let your old paradigms get in the way, and trust the universe to deliver. I know because I manifested a flight on a private jet with Bob Proctor.

This was during a year when I traveled to many conferences (something I do regularly to sharpen my saw and learn more). I enrolled in an event in Toronto, where I signed up to hear Bob speak. At almost the same time, I was already signed up for a training with Bob in Vegas. I had become a leading consultant in the Proctor Gallagher Institute, working with Bob Proctor, and wanted to take advantage of as much training as possible.

I had no idea how I would get from Toronto to Vegas in time, but I knew I would. Because Bob would be at both events, I thought, *wouldn't it be cool to fly with Bob on his jet?*

For most of us, that's the kind of idea where you say to yourself, "That's crazy. You can't do that." But I didn't listen to that negativity in my head. I imagined myself on that jet and let it go.

A couple of months before those two events, I was at another conference in Toronto. I showed up early for one training, and when I got to the training, there were just a few people there, and Bob was at the front of the room getting his slides ready. Normally, we all leave Bob alone at that time because we know he is thinking through his presentation and getting himself centered. But I had the strongest urge to go talk to him before the audience came into the room, so I crossed the room and said hello. Bob said hello to me and then asked me, "Where did I see you last?"

I told him I'd been at a prior event of his, and he asked if I was going to the ones in Toronto and Vegas in a couple of months. The words just flowed out of me; I didn't think it through; I just went with my gut. "Yes," I said, "I'm just trying to work out the logistics."

Just like that, he said, "Why don't you fly with me?" And boom, I had an invitation to ride on his jet. A friend of mine happened by, and she declared she was going with me, even though she didn't have an invitation.

Afterward, I emailed Bob's assistant every once in a while to tell her I was grateful for the trip and ask if there was anything I could do for him. I was letting my nerves and old paradigms get to me and make me feel insecure.

Then I stopped myself and said, "No more." I closed my eyes and held onto that vision of myself on his plane—held it there with sheer will because the doubts were so strong. The old me wanted to email Bob's assistant and say, "Hey, I don't want him to feel pressured to take me. If he's changed his mind, that's okay." The new me held onto that vision and didn't send that doubting email.

> My one bold move created
> a snowball of opportunities
> and opened amazing new doors.

A month later, Bob's assistant asked me for my passport information and mentioned they were holding a contest for the last seat on the plane. They had a drawing at the event—and the name that was drawn was my friend's. We all flew in style from Toronto to Vegas and back again, masterminding the whole way. What an incredible experience, which only happened because I used my will to cement that image I had created in my imagination.

MENTAL FACULTY THREE: PERCEPTION

One Saturday morning, my husband and I started arguing about cleaning the house, of all things. At the time, I was going through grad school and taking care of my terminally ill father. I was working, studying, caretaking—essentially stretched to the max. That insatiable desire to always be achieving more, doing more, buying more was driven by this inner belief that I wasn't enough. I wasn't smart enough. I wasn't thin enough. I wasn't talented enough—whatever enough there was, I didn't have it.

On this particular Saturday, he started cleaning the house because I was working (back then, I worked all the time). I started to make up a story in my head that my husband thought I was lazy, and he didn't think I was doing enough because I wasn't helping him clean the house. In my head, I spun a tale about everything I was doing that would prove I wasn't lazy. When I said something to him about cleaning the house, I had all that negative mental energy already going, and I had an attitude that would cause us to argue.

My perception of his simple act of cleaning the house was that he was doing it because he thought I was lazy. I had this whole story going on inside my head that *wasn't even true*, which I realized after we talked. It was all in how I perceived what was happening.

> When you change the way you look at things,
> the things you look at change.
>
> WAYNE DYER

Around this time, I went to a three-day seminar that amped up our self-awareness. We started peeling back the layers like an onion and digging down to see what made us tick. I realized that my old paradigms were affecting how I perceived what was happening around me. When I came home from the seminar, I noticed my husband had cleaned the house. I thanked him for doing this instead of listening to my "not good enough" story.

The three-day seminar helped me make a shift, not because my husband changed, but because I did. I changed how I perceived him and his contribution to our household. That, in turn, shifted how I responded to him. I was no longer in reaction mode; I wasn't acting on my deep internal belief of not being enough. I had shifted my perspective to one of gratitude, and it changed everything in our interactions.

MENTAL FACULTY FOUR: INTUITION

We all have intuition, that little voice guiding us along; that "feeling" you get when you just know something is right or wrong. It's that voice of wisdom telling you to bring an umbrella when it's a sunny day outside. You think it's crazy (and everyone around you might, too), but later the skies open up, and you're really glad you brought that umbrella.

I liken intuition to a GPS. If you just sit in the driveway, your GPS will not provide you with instructions or guidance. You have to take one action step so you can be guided to your destination. That one action step leads to the next, and the next, until you are at your destination.

When you are in harmony with what you desire, you can feel your intuition guiding you. But when you are bombarded by the circumstances around you, and you're stuck in analysis paralysis, that's your fear talking. Just listen to your gut for a second—are you feeling joyous and excited or anxious and scared?

When I started running my own business, I hired a coach to create Facebook ads. I'd been doing well on my own but was too busy to keep doing the ads, so I hired this "expert" who started doing things the opposite of how I did them. Something in the back of my head made me question his tactics. *Why is he redoing this? This is working; we should be using this momentum.* Instead of speaking up and listening to my intuition, I let fear of being wrong keep me from making changes.

> My intuition was telling me to ask questions, but I was letting my fear of not knowing enough and not understanding tech, and wanting to be nice and agreeable get in the way of what my intuition was screaming at me to do. I lost so much money because I didn't listen.

To let your intuition tell you what to do, you have to quiet your mind and stop listening to the fear. Quiet your mind, either with meditation or just by going somewhere solitary, and stop the negative churning thoughts.

Try it right now. Sit still for a minute. Just pause, and ask yourself these questions:

> *What am I feeling right now?*
> *Why am I feeling this way?*
> *What do I need right now?*

Don't ignore any of the answers, and be truly honest with yourself. Are you feeling anxious or calm? Are you worried and stressed or excited about the next step? Next, think about your desired result and start taking inspired action that causes you to feel calm and centered. If I had done this small exercise, I would have saved so much heartache and drama later on. All I needed to do was pause so that I would have asked better questions at the moment and stopped letting fear drive the car.

MENTAL FACULTY FIVE: MEMORY

Chances are that you're using your memory, another of our mental faculties, all wrong, and it's keeping you stuck creating the same results. A lot of us look at our past and allow it to dictate what we create in the future. For example, if you have a past mistake or past hurt, you might be allowing that to dictate what you think you can do.

In reality, we have it backward because there's no limit to what you're capable of achieving. The only limits are the ones that we impose on ourselves. That's where our memories of past failures come into play and make us not trust ourselves. This is part of the concept of sunk cost bias, where people will engage in projects and things that are going poorly (and they believe, based on past experience, will fail) but they stick with it because they have already sunk money and ego into it.

Don't be afraid of saying, *Wait, this isn't working*, then redirect or pivot. Then learn to use your memory constructively.

Remember, energy attracts like energy. To create positive energy with your future goals, you need to reach back in your memory to a time when you felt the way you imagine yourself feeling when you hit that C goal. Maybe you were proud of yourself or just felt carefree and joyful. It might be a time in your life when you felt like you were just winning and on top of the world. Bring that memory into sharp focus. Now use that feeling to create the image of something that you want to have in the future. I call this creating future memories.

What you're doing is pairing a positive memory with a desired outcome. For example, if you want to start a business and your reason for doing that is to give back to other people, then try picturing a time when you were giving back and feeling good about that. Then morph that into an image of the future you doing that when you have achieved your goal. Feel the joy of it and the gratitude of it right now. Every night before you go to bed, do this exercise, either in writing or in your mind, and stop letting your past hold you back.

MENTAL FACULTY SIX: REASON

Reason is a great mental faculty to have, but like memory, we are using it wrong. We are using our reason to keep ourselves stuck in place instead of using it to free ourselves to do so much more. My mother is elderly, and the people at her assisted living facility keep warning her not to do this or that because she'll fall, and if she keeps falling, she will have to leave the facility and go to skilled care. They have instilled all these negative associations (if I do this, I will fall, and I will have to leave) and have made her a nervous wreck who's afraid to move.

We become our thoughts. Dr. Thurmond Fleet, a chiropractor, did a study on this many years ago, where he realized that patients could heal themselves if they could envision that healing. He drew a stick figure representing the conscious mind (the top half of the head) and, beneath that, the subconscious mind. Whatever we get emotionally connected with in our conscious mind becomes embedded in our subconscious mind (I'm afraid of falling, and my subconscious mind will warn me not to move). The conscious mind, however, can accept or reject information. The subconscious mind only accepts what you feed it with emotion, like a garden. You can either feed it weeds or flower seeds.

Those subconscious thoughts and beliefs move your body into action (or not taking action). That action causes a reaction—which is your result. Are your results not what you wanted? Are you not moving forward in the direction you want to go? Then chances are you are not letting reason be used in the right way. Instead of having fear about paying the bills (and being in that scarcity mentality, which becomes a fear of not having enough in your subconscious), look at history where you have succeeded and reason that you will succeed again. Feel that emotion of success, and connect it with this moment to start attaching positive emotions to your subconscious.

Everything is energy. To succeed when things get tough, come back to matching your energy frequency with what you want, not with negativity.

If you're in a scarcity mentality, you are pushing away the thing you want most. If you are feeling desperate, you will show that desperation in everything you do.

Remember the Law of Attraction? You attract what you focus on. Don't focus on the negative or what you don't have. Instead, go back to the six mental faculties and visual ease and flow in achieving your goal. Have an energy of abundance, and believe in the strengths and successes you have already accomplished and will again.

Whichever energy you choose to embrace, it will have a snowball effect. It is up to you to choose whether that snowball will be filled with negativity or positive, conscious thoughts.

CHAPTER 9
KNOW WHO IS THE REAL PROBLEM

You can dream big goals and take steps toward those goals, but you're never going to achieve what you want if you are the one holding you back. You end up self-sabotaging the very things you want most in the world because you aren't changing what is happening inside yourself.

The results that you are achieving are a direct reflection of the image of yourself you are holding. Improve the image, and the improvement will automatically be reflected in your results.

SANDY GALLAGHER

Imagine holding a cup of coffee. Someone comes along and bumps into you, and the coffee spills. You might tell yourself *that person made me spill my coffee.* But that's not what happened. You spilled your coffee because there was coffee in the cup. If the cup had been empty and someone had bumped into you, nothing would have spilled.

You are going to hit bumps along the way. The road will never be completely smooth. If something or someone bumps into you—what will spill out of you? What are you putting in your mental cup?

Remember the quote from Wayne Dyer earlier in the book about the orange? Think about what you have inside you and what will emerge if you are squeezed (put under pressure).

Are you filling your cup with joy, gratitude, and humility, or is it chock-full of harsh words, fears, and complaints? Because you choose what is in your cup, and if you choose negativity, that's what will come out whenever you hit a setback.

TAKE LEADERSHIP OF YOURSELF

It's vital that you take 100% responsibility for everything you create, including the thoughts in your head. In previous chapters, we talked about how what we attract and create comes not from what we want but from *who we are*. Who we are is thanks to all those paradigms running the show. They are making up our self-image, how we see the world around us, how we react to what happens, and by extension, the results we create in life.

Look at the Gallagher quote above and think about it in terms of the paradigms in your head. If you have a lot of insecurities about your abilities and self, you will unwittingly see yourself as someone who doesn't deserve that great life. If your paradigms say you are reaching too high or don't have the skills to do A, B, and C, then those doubts will come along and sabotage you.

We have many false beliefs about ourselves, our capabilities, leadership ability, and whether we see ourselves as successful entrepreneurs. Those beliefs can block us from seeing the reality of who we are. They can build up a lack of confidence that we might not even be aware of.

That's why that mental Kevlar is so important. Understanding things on an intellectual level doesn't change your external circumstances until you rebuild that internal image of yourself.

Self-sabotage is a real thing, something even I am guilty of from time to time. Recently, my group coaching mastermind gave everyone individual assignments designed to get us out of our comfort zones. My assignment was to go to a public place like a mall and convince at least twelve strangers to allow me to create a spontaneous love poem for their significant other. That kind of extroverted behavior is completely the opposite of who I normally am, and I freaked out a little bit inside.

My initial gut reaction was to enroll a friend to come with me. She's much more boisterous than me, and I knew her laughter would be infectious and encourage people to talk to us. She's 100% an extrovert, whereas I see myself as more of an introvert, someone who feels comfortable being in the midst of the excitement, not creating it. Many of my friends are more gregarious, outgoing, and fearless, being their full authentic selves.

But I knew that bringing someone along would only defeat the purpose of getting me out of my comfort zone. So I went to the mall and stood in the food court, holding my notebook and wondering who I would approach for my first round of love poems. I saw a mother and daughter who appeared harmless and nice, so I went up to them and offered to share some love and joy by creating a spontaneous poem. They said that was nice, but they weren't interested. I approached an older gentleman who said no right off the bat. Then I went into a shop I frequent, and the cashier also said no to me.

I realized that something in my method was not working, but I wasn't sure what it was. I went home, feeling dejected. As I thought about the day, I realized that I had been coming at this all wrong. I was doing this exercise because I had to, not because I was coming from a place of love and wholeness for others.

A couple of days later, I had to visit the VA. I decided I would shower everyone I met with love, from the guy who waved my car in to the woman behind the desk. I gave them each a poem of love, not expecting anything in return. The guy who waved my car through the gate was so inspired that he gave me a short poem in return. It was amazing. There I was, inspiring love and connection first thing on a Monday morning.

What was different? The answer: what I was filling my head with. Instead of thinking, *this isn't something I do; this isn't me,* I decided that spreading love, connection, and joy was a part of me. I adopted that as part of who I am and began doing it more often in all areas of my life. That new thinking manifested in smiles and gratitude in return.

> Instead of seeing this task as a chore, I saw it as something that was aligned with the kind of person I was and the person I wanted to be more often.

THE SNEAKY PARADIGM YO-YO

Your paradigms are always trying to keep you from getting outside that comfortable spot you have created in your life. When you change your behavior without changing how you see yourself on the inside, your paradigm will notice the disconnect and drag you back to home base.

When several people told me no on my first attempt at the love poem task, I felt rejected, and it impacted my mood that day, even though I knew it wasn't personal. Maxwell Maltz's book *Psycho-Cybernetics* talks about how our self-image is like a cybernetic mechanism. As a plastic surgeon, he wanted to study why people who had plastic surgery said the results didn't measure up to their expectations. He realized there was a correlation between their self-image and how they perceived their physical bodies.

A person can set a goal, and the mechanism of the body and mind will move toward that goal, whether that be in a positive or negative light. If you think negatively about the goal, the results won't be what you expected. For example, if you go into a restaurant expecting lousy service or bad food, the meal will live up to those expectations.

If you go into a race expecting to feel tired and lag behind the leader, you will most certainly do those very things. However, going into either of those situations anticipating and believing in a positive outcome will greatly enhance the experience and, most of all, your perception of it.

My paradigm tried several times to drag me back to my comfort zone. I started overanalyzing the task—is it twelve individuals or twelve couples? Then I listed reasons it was impossible—I don't have the time; this doesn't make sense for me to do.

However, once I shifted my self-image to see myself as the kind of person who talks to strangers and gives them a happy gift, it shifted my behavior. My belief that I could do it and receive a positive response from people became clear in the way I spoke, held myself, and approached other people. The reaction from people was night and day.

How we do one thing is how we do everything. This lesson is applicable to anything that we do where we are not feeling comfortable. It gives us an opportunity to show ourselves that our limiting beliefs are simply not true. Be willing to be unreasonable and to take risks.

For example, take someone who wants to lose weight and get in shape. He buys the books, gets the videos, hires a trainer, joins a gym, and fills his cupboards with healthy options. For a couple of weeks, maybe even a month, things go well. Then suddenly, the person finds himself back on the couch. It's not because he didn't have the tools to get fit. He knew what to do and how to become a fit person, but his cybernetic self and all its paradigms sensed him deviating from the plan (maybe he skipped a day at the gym or indulged in dessert a couple of times) and pulled him right back into his comfort zone. Your brain is designed to keep you comfortable.

It wasn't enough to change his behavior. He also had to build a new self-image around the person he wanted to become—a self-image that saw him as a fit, healthy person.

If you want to become a leader, you have to believe that you are someone that others want to follow. That you are a great communicator. That you are worthy of being a leader. It's the same with anything you want to create in your life.

THE IMPACT OF IMPOSTER SYNDROME

The thief of comparison, of feeling like you don't deserve what someone else has achieved, can steal so many great opportunities from you. When I was caught in the rat race, I deflected or pushed away job opportunities in my career because I didn't think I was good enough to advance to those levels. In my mind, a leader in the military was a boisterous man, not a woman like me. When I was asked to take on a leadership role, I stopped it from happening, not once, not twice, but three times because I didn't believe I could be a leader. Yet I had the resume, the capabilities, and the support of others who recognized my leadership abilities. I was comparing myself to other people and finding myself lacking over and over again. I wondered when the other shoe would drop, and people would realize the real me was a mess.

Even though I was doing the work, getting promoted, and being successful, I was miserable because I didn't feel worthy of any of it. As a result, I wasn't living and serving at my highest level. I was always looking outside myself for the awards and accolades to fill my cup and prove to myself that I was worthy and good enough.

Most of our time is spent thinking about things that have happened in the past or things that haven't even happened. We worry, obsess, and overanalyze. *What if they expect me to do it again, and I can't? What if I fail this time? What if I'm not good enough to do the job?*

> Here's a simple truth: You don't have control over any of that; you only have control over the *now*.

All those worries would manifest inside me whenever I was in a meeting. I knew I should speak up and share my thoughts, but my palms would get sweaty, my face would become flushed, and my voice was choked. I was suffocating my voice. Before I knew it, the moment would pass. It wasn't until I started to allow myself to dream and believe that I could do these things that everything began to change.

CHANGING YOUR RESULTS

Creating different results is an *inside* job. If you are looking outside yourself for validation that you are capable, strong, and worthy, you'll never find enough validation to change your paradigms. You have to work on that from the inside out.

Start with building an image in your mind of the person you want to be. How would that person act? Speak? Walk? Dress? Interact? If you struggle to see that image, look at someone you admire. Don't compare yourself, simply write down the attributes they have that you admire. Maybe somebody is charismatic or well-spoken or has a great deal of confidence. You can adopt—or borrow—those attributes until you feel the same about yourself.

Start to write those attributes you want to have into your script. See yourself as that confident leader, a strong communicator, or whatever it may be. Build that image in your mind, and through repetition, you will eventually see yourself like that all the time. Once that image is embedded in your subconscious mind, you will exude those qualities, and other people will start to see you that way too.

For me, reaching out to those twelve people had nothing to do with the goal of talking to them and writing a spontaneous love poem. What mattered was who I became on the way to achieving that goal. Even if I only spoke to three people, as long as I felt good, and had the courage and the spontaneity, I had changed myself to be better and stronger. That is the journey.

Here are some questions you can ask yourself today to get a sense of where you fall regarding your image of yourself. Take some time to think about these and write down truthful answers:

- What do you think about yourself?

- How do you feel about yourself?

- Do you have a positive image of yourself, or is there room for improvement?

- Is your self-image empowering?

- What's the inner dialogue you have with and about yourself most often?

- What are some qualities you like about yourself?

- How can you bring these qualities out more with people at work and in your life?

- Who do you admire and why?

- What are some attributes you would like to adopt from them?

- Which one attribute can you adopt this week?

- Take the C goal you created in Chapter 6. Write a life script of who you are in this goal, who do you get to become, and how does it feel being this new self?

Because the mind thinks in pictures, it's important to visualize the person you want to become. What do you look like? What do your physical surroundings look like? Everything is created first in our mind, then in physical form, and this new self is no different. Write this image down and repeat it daily to yourself, embedding it in your subconscious.

Anytime you move up the ladder of life or career, the person you were isn't the person who will get you to the next level. All along the journey, there have been shifts and alterations, whether you realize it or not. I'm asking you to make your inside match the accomplished you on the outside. Start making those bigger mind shifts right now and begin living your best life right away.

CHAPTER 10

CREATE AN ATTITUDE OF SUCCESS

Your attitude can have a major impact on how successful your efforts are in everything you do, but especially in achieving your goal. Because your attitude is the composite of your thoughts, feelings, and actions, it pulls together everything in your mind and reflects in your choices. We all know how a bad attitude can make a difficult situation worse, but did you know it can also take something positive and quickly take it down a negative route?

In this chapter, I'll share the go-to quick exercise I use whenever I need to shift my thoughts or how I feel in a particular situation. It works on an individual level and is also a great exercise for a team.

Attitude ties together everything we have already talked about—our current self-image, our image of the person we want to become, our goal, and our mental Kevlar. When you struggle to see the path ahead or a way out of your current situation, your attitude is the biggest key to changing direction.

Bob Proctor once said—and I'm paraphrasing this— that attitude is such a prevalent word in our society. We are told that we'd have better jobs or relationships if we had a better attitude. Doctors will tell their patients that after all the medical options have been exhausted, it's up to the patient's attitude to positively impact their health. Attitude is so important, yet we know so little about it.

You may think you have a positive attitude. For instance, you're in a job that doesn't fulfill you or a relationship that isn't working. You can buck up and be happy—but that's not a positive attitude. That's essentially resigning yourself to a shitty situation. It's you settling for less than you desire and deserve.

Settling isn't what we want. Yes, we want
to be satisfied, fulfilled, and grateful, but
settling isn't the path to growth.

You don't have to grit your teeth and get through the
day. You can change your attitude (as we talked about
earlier) and change your future.

START WITH YOUR THOUGHTS

Creative power and energy flow through us and to us.
This creative power has no form; it's not positive or
negative; it's simply expressed as a vibration through
our gestures, words, and writing. However, it can have
a major impact on our thinking and our results.

We take in information through our five senses, and
we think in pictures. Those thoughts go straight to our
conscious mind. When those thoughts and information
come into our minds, we have the ability to accept or
reject that idea. For example, you might walk into a
meeting and see one of the people at the conference
table scowling and drumming his fingers on the table.

You have the choice to think: *He's already annoyed with
me and won't listen to what I have to say.* What will be
the result of those thoughts? You'll immediately be

anxious, probably rush through your presentation, and give off an air of insecurity.

What if you refused to accept that thought instead? We never know what's going on in someone else's mind. Maybe that guy has a late project, and he's stressed about delivering on time. Maybe he's had too much caffeine, and he's feeling jittery. Maybe he's worried about being laid off or had a fight with his spouse. You have absolutely no idea if his scowl is personal. You can choose to reject the thought that he's already annoyed with you, then get yourself into an attitude of success and present with authority and confidence.

Anytime an idea or thought makes it past the stopgap in your conscious mind and is internalized with emotion (as in our example, a thought of imminent rejection that makes you anxious and unsure), your subconscious mind doesn't have the ability to reject that notion. Anything you allow into your conscious mind with feeling becomes embedded in your subconscious mind. That feeling becomes the vibration and energy within you. Think about it—if you meet someone who is struggling with negative or angry thoughts, you can feel that energy coming off them. If they are having positive thoughts, you can feel that positive energy aligning with their feelings.

MAKE YOUR ATTITUDE REFLECT IN YOUR ACTIONS

When an idea is impressed on the subconscious mind, it becomes imprinted, and that moves your body into action. If you got burned by a hot stove once, that painful memory becomes imprinted on your subconscious mind, and the next time you are around a hot stove, you put some distance between yourself and the flame.

This also happens when you have conflict in your mind, but in a different way. If your mind is in a conflict between what you are thinking and feeling, your mind is in a state of confusion. You might be thinking that you want to take a big risk with your business, but you are feeling unsure and insecure, and when that happens, your confusion manifests in your actions and surroundings. Your car becomes a trash can. Your office is a cluttered mess. Your thoughts aren't well formed. When you try to communicate an idea to someone, the words come out botched. Why? Because you aren't in alignment with your thoughts, feelings, and beliefs, and that is manifesting in your actions.

If you, deep down inside, don't believe you're capable or worthy of the success that is coming your way, that will manifest in procrastination, self-sabotage, and doubt. You won't carry yourself like someone who believes they can achieve big things. Your voice won't hold that authority when you speak.

Your results will be subpar, and if you allow your attitude to get in the way, it will reinforce those negative beliefs. *I knew I couldn't do it. I'm not good enough. I don't deserve that. I'm not as talented as the other people.*

You'll feel all these negative emotions to go with the thoughts, imprinting on your subconscious and creating a vicious circle that can be hard to escape. You have to start with changing your attitude about yourself, your abilities, and your success, and couple that with positive feelings because your subconscious mind will be imprinted with can-do beliefs. And those who believe they can do—do.

THE ATTITUDE-ADJUSTMENT EXERCISE

This is an exercise that will help you shift your attitude and energy, which will result in a change in your results. It's truly magic, and I encourage you to try it.

Think about a situation that's not going well, something that you want to improve. Write it down on a piece of paper or in a journal, using as much detail as possible. Try drawing Dr. Thurman Fleet's stick figure we talked about in a previous chapter. Write *Thoughts* across the top half of the head and *Feelings* on the lower half. Write *Actions* along the body and draw arrows connecting the three.

Ask yourself what thoughts you are having about this situation, and write down the answers. If you can go deeper, try to transport yourself inside that situation. For instance, what thoughts do you have when you dread seeing someone you don't want to talk to? Maybe your thoughts are: *This always ends in an argument. I don't want to go.*

As you revisit the situation, think about what feelings are coming up for you (and write those down). Are you feeling tightness in your chest, is your heart pounding, is your neck tight? Are you feeling frustrated, angry, or scared? Write all of this down *without judging yourself.*

Now write down the actions that you have been taking to deal with this situation up until now—have you been avoiding the person, losing your temper, or procrastinating on the meeting?

Across from the actions, I want you to write down the results you are getting in a bulleted list. Are you seeing the correlation between your actions and your results?

For example, early on, I wasn't getting a lot of sales. My calls were ending in "no" answers, and I was getting rejected. These were the results of my actions, which were related to my feelings and thoughts. When I saw how those three things impacted my results, I was able to change what I was doing and transform my results.

Your results are a reflection of what's going on inside of you. When your thoughts, feelings, and actions are all in alignment (i.e., your attitude), your results will improve. Be honest with yourself during this exercise, and don't judge yourself.

A key question to ask is:
***Is this situation controlling your thinking,
or are you controlling the situation?***

If you are getting rejected in sales calls, not getting the raise, not earning the income you want, or not being received by other people the way you want to be received, that is all telling you that there is a disconnect between what you think and how you feel. Results show you what's going on inside you. Go back to that exercise about the difficult situation and ask yourself: What things would be better to just let go, reject, or allow to roll off your shoulders?

Don't worry—I won't leave you sitting in your own crap in this chapter. There is a way to turn it all around and change things so you can go to the next level. We'll do this exercise again, but with a different focus, based on the mental faculties we discussed in previous chapters.

> Write down the situation again, except this time, write about it as if it has unfolded the way you want it to. Add as many details as you can. Allow your imagination to run with this do-over version of the situation.

What thoughts are you having about this new version? *I'm grateful for this opportunity. I'm showing up as my best self. I'm going to leave them with an impression of increase. One more no is just getting me closer to a yes. I'm excited to share what I have to offer. How can I best serve this person?*

As you read this new version and the thoughts you could be thinking, write down how you are feeling inside. Empowered? Excited? Motivated? Joyful? And most of all, in control of you, instead of the situation controlling you?

Now that you are in that elevated vibration state, write down what actions you feel inspired to take right now. These three things right there—that is your new attitude.

When I did that band performance I mentioned in a previous chapter, I was nervous before I got on the stage, so sure the audience would see my big, red head and start laughing because I wasn't the rapper they expected. And it went exactly as I expected because that was my attitude. I felt like a failure. That started chipping away at my confidence, and after two shows like that, I decided I'd had enough.

Instead of quitting, I decided to joke with one of the kids who were teasing me and turn it around playfully. To go into it with an attitude of having fun and effectively communicating with the kids. When I did that, I felt edgy and powerful. I was able to redirect my irritation and nerves into a powerful persona. All of that attitude and energy came through. When the lights shone on me during the third show, I performed with confidence. The audience responded with a different, positive vibe as well.

There was a great give and take of energy, which brought more joy to what I was doing. At the end of the show, we split the audience in half between me and another bandmate and had a chanting competition. The kids on my team went nuts when it was their turn, and in the end, everyone had fun. I felt pride in my job and no longer felt like I was the weakest link on the team.

You can apply this exercise to all areas of your life. What situations are you going through in your finances, business, health, social life, and relationships? What are your thoughts, feelings, actions, and results? Are they in alignment? Can you imagine a better outcome?

If you have a team that is struggling, do this exercise as a team and help them craft some more empowering thoughts, feelings, and actions. Help them envision the results this change of attitude can manifest.

You can shift your attitude in a moment by doing this, even if you do it in your head. You can pause for a few minutes before you walk into a meeting or presentation and change your entire attitude, as well as the outcome of that moment.

Here's the thing—knowing better doesn't mean you'll do better. Repeating affirmations all day doesn't make them come true. Unless you are emotionally involved and connected with what you are affirming, it won't work. Look at your results—they are the barometer of what you believe deep down inside yourself. They will tell you if you aren't in alignment. Work on the exercise in this chapter on a regular basis, and you'll begin imprinting positive thoughts and feelings on your subconscious mind and will start to see much better results from your every action.

CHAPTER 11

FORM A FOUNDATION OF CORE VALUES

Have you ever met someone or dealt with a company that said they believed in something, but their actions didn't match those values? How did you feel? Disappointed? Angry? Fooled?

Your branding has to match your values because if it doesn't, nothing works, and all your efforts can come tumbling down as quickly as a house of cards on a windy day. None of the things we have talked about in this book—goal setting, manifesting, paradigm-shifting, and intentional actions—will work if the core values (the foundation of who you are as a person) don't match your dreams.

> What are your values? Are you walking the walk and not just talking the talk about what you believe?

When your values aren't aligned with your actions, there is no amount of manifesting that will bring your goals to life. That's not to say that you can't change to become that person you dream of being—but you have to be just as intentional in living up to those values as you are with everything else in your world.

CREATE VALUE-DRIVEN HABITS

You've done all this work, figured out what you want, realized what you don't want, and now have the clarity to move past the mental roadblocks standing in your way. Now it's all about creating the value-driven habits that build your credibility and trust with your clients and the people around you.

Take a moment to write down ten things that are important to you, whether that's giving back or supporting a particular cause, or being honest and open with others. These values form the foundation of who you will be going forward. You might not be all those things yet, but you can be by going back through the steps in this book and applying all those principles to cultivating the values that are important to you.

> The skills you learn to shift your paradigms, create C-level goals, and take the intentional actions that lead to your dream can be applied to any part of your life and person.

Maintain that same level of focus and intention as you have with your goals, because every time you do that, you are telling the hippocampus (the data storage part of your brain) that this thought or action is important. That stores it in your long and short-term memory, ready to be recalled when needed. For instance, if you want to be a more positive person and spread positivity to those around you, becoming that person can take a lot of effort, especially if you tend to think negatively. However, every time you take a negative thought and reframe it in a positive way, you are training your brain to think differently. Eventually, you don't have to do it consciously because it all happens automatically in your subconscious.

PRACTICE DAILY

When you first create a C-goal, you spend time writing it down, reading it, and repeating it to yourself. You can do the same thing with your values. Anytime you have a change you want to implement in yourself, develop a regular practice to recall that information. Write it down (I am a positive person) and say that to yourself in the mirror multiple times a day.

James Clear talks about habit stacking in his book, *Atomic Habits*. That's the idea of tying something you are already doing to a new habit you want to implement. For example, if you take the dog for a walk every morning before work, make that the time you speak your daily habits aloud to yourself. Or make it a game and name a new value habit every time you turn a corner or pour a cup of coffee. Whatever it is, tie these new habits to ones that are already engaging your brain (because doing this while you are sitting on the couch watching TV doesn't work that well).

Break the task into smaller tasks. Maybe your new goal is to be someone who doesn't hit the snooze button in the morning and instead becomes someone who gets right up and runs five miles every day. That's a big leap from couch potato to daily runner. The first day you skip, you'll break the new habit and be right back where you started. It's completely demotivating.

Instead, start with creating muscle memory. "When my alarm goes off in the morning, I will put my feet on the floor." Experts say it takes twenty-one days to create a new habit, so every single day for twenty-one days, as soon as the alarm goes off, sit up and put your feet on the floor and get up. You don't have to run five miles—you can put on your shoes and walk or run one mile, then work up to two, and so on. The point is to build the muscle memory that creates that habit until it becomes a core value.

Create the habits that lead to the dream,
vision, and ideas that you have for yourself.

These kinds of actions create the triggers, or mental cues and links, to the new habit. The alarm goes off = putting your feet on the floor. Putting your feet on the floor = lacing up your running shoes. Lacing up your running shoes = going outside. Going outside = putting on some motivational music. Motivational music = starting your run.

This may seem very elementary, and it is. However, most people don't do these simple habit stacks that can transform their lives. If your vision of yourself is a healthy, fit, athletic person, you have to create the habits that lead to that vision, one after another. We often have big, grand ideas, but when it comes time to lock those ideas in and implement them, we fall short because we haven't built the foundation that gets us there.

BUILD IN REWARDS

We talked earlier in the book about building a mastermind group that challenges you, encourages you to get out of your comfort zone, and makes you try a little harder. You don't have to have a mastermind group for everything you want to do, but you should have some kind of social interaction as a reward system for achieving your new goals. Whether this group is a mastermind, a success posse, or just a group of friends who gets together for regular high fives, build your exterior network because they help you build internal fortitude.

Back to the running example. If you run with a few friends once a week and all exchange high-fives after a difficult hot summer run, you are elevating your oxytocin levels (the reward center in your brain) through social interaction and touch. That high five is creating energy behind your goal, which is helping it be fulfilled. It's telling your brain this new goal is a great idea and builds positivity around the goal.

You can also create self-motivation. I believe that journaling and celebrating even the smallest of wins is crucial. Rewards are motivating, period. Your reward doesn't have to be a slice of chocolate cake—it can be a simple "good job!" that you say aloud to yourself after you finish a tough task or build twenty-one days of a new habit.

Use only positive rewards. Numerous studies have shown that negative, fear-based systems don't work as well as positive reward systems. Telling yourself something like: *I suck, I didn't do as well as I could have* is detrimental to your inner belief systems. Try instead: *I did a great job. I got out there and tried my hardest. I'm on my way to being a great [whatever you want to be].*

It also gets you emotionally involved with your values. Remember when we did the C-goal visualization earlier in the book, and talked about feeling the emotions of having that goal become a reality? You can do the same with your values. Feel the self-satisfaction, joy, and self-love that becoming that person gives you. Feel good about yourself, as silly as that sounds, because it works. Your emotional connection to your goals goes back to that reward center. When your brain perceives that this is a good feeling, it will want more of that.

CHANGE HOW YOU SEE YOURSELF

This goes back to that mental conditioning. If you see yourself as a negative person or see yourself as someone who is out of shape, you will continue to perpetuate that feeling, even if you win awards for writing inspiring poetry or finishing a marathon. You can change any behavior with willpower. But to carve out new neural pathways and lock in this new persona, you have to change the way you think about and see yourself.

Earlier, we talked about the power of affirmation and visualization. Olympic athletes use these two skills to help their performance. They visualize a successful result over and over again, walking themselves mentally through every step in the process, from getting up in the morning to crossing the finish line. They tell themselves they can do it. They are constantly self-affirming. When you use affirmations and visualization, you are setting up mental and verbal cues that go along with your habits, creating that powerful mind-action connection that leads to success.

> Imagine how you would feel if you did what you said you would do. How much more confidence would you have in yourself? How would you view yourself? How would you feel about this new self who is putting themselves first and getting things done?

If you want to be the person who saves one-third of every paycheck toward retirement and dream vacations, but you are currently living paycheck to paycheck, take a minute to think about how you would feel if you saw your savings account balance increasing every single month. You'd feel confident, trustworthy, and amazing, right? Make that feeling into a daily affirmation: *I am so happy and grateful that I follow through on what I say I will do. I love seeing the balance in my bank account grow.*

No amount of manifesting will overcome not believing in yourself as a person who has these values because imposter syndrome will sneak in and reawaken those old paradigms, dragging you back to where you were before. If you are struggling to attain your goals and feel like something isn't right, then it's very likely that you haven't done the belief work yet, and you are struggling to believe you are this person. That's where it helps to have other people in your corner who can help reinforce those beliefs.

MAKE YOUR VALUES MATCH YOUR ACTIONS

The values you choose for yourself shouldn't be shallow. They should be deep, core values that fuel who you are as a person every single day. You don't have to wait to become that person—you can *be* that person today.

> Do you want to be someone who is focused on service to others? Then operate with integrity. If you want to be a philanthropist, be a good human being in all areas of your life. Start acting like that person in every choice you make.

With your company, the branding you are putting out should match the internal actions. If you say you value teamwork but only reward individualistic behaviors, you are sending a mixed message. Do you say you value open communication but immediately squash any opposing viewpoints? When you aren't living your company values, you breed mistrust among the employees.

Reward the people who are living by the company vision, even if it's something as simple as a "great job" or a lunch purchased by the boss. The goal is to keep people motivated to stay aligned with the company's vision and values.

If you are part of a team, check in with the overall team goal every day as an individual and as a team. It's too easy to get caught up in complacency and assume you are doing well when you aren't. Get a read from the other team members on whether they think you are adhering to the values you set out at the beginning.

> The Reticular Activating System is always looking for evidence that supports your values, so talk about them, remember moments that showcase them, and reward yourself or other people who espouse them.

It's so easy to get off track because those paradigms are hardwired into our brains. There's a guy on YouTube who spent eight months learning how to ride a backward bicycle (when you turn the steering wheel left, the bike goes right, and when you turn it right, the bike goes left). Every day, he spent a few minutes learning that new way of riding a bike and managed to conquer it. When someone gave him a regular bike to use, it only took him twenty minutes to go back to riding the old way. That's how quickly your paradigms can return and undo all the great progress you have made. Create the habits, practice them regularly, become emotionally attached to being that person, and reward yourself for every step forward.

You don't have to spend hours and hours on this. The guy who learned to ride the backward bike spent five minutes a day practicing. That's all you need to remind yourself of your values and goals and celebrate your wins. Building the values you want your company and yourself to exhibit is the final step in achieving everything you ever wanted and living life to the utmost.

Remember, everything is created twice—once in your imagination and once in physical form. Imagine it and make it happen!

TWELVE STEPS TO HAVING IT ALL

We've talked about many concepts in this book and thrown a lot of information at you in a short time. I wanted to create a one-stop guide sheet to get from where you are now, stuck in the rat race, to the life of your dreams. Print this out and hang it by your mirror. Make notes, adding your goals. Use it as a basis for building the habits that will take you, intentional action by intentional action, to where you want to go.

1. Know What You Want

Are you where you want to be right now? If not, then the best place to start is right here, right now. This is the beginning of your new life. Start with figuring out what you want that to look like. A four-day work week? A certain amount of money in the bank? Time to go to the kids' soccer games? A company that's earning nine figures a year? Write down that vision.

2. Act as If You're Efficient

You don't have a lack of time—you have a lack of efficiency. We all have twenty-four hours in a day, but many of us allow time-wasters to suck up those hours. Whether it's micromanaging, a lack of clarity, busy tasks, or simple fear, name your time-wasters. Once you've done that, make a list of more efficient ways to use that time. How would a person who is efficient and successful use those same hours?

3. Overcome Your "Lack" of Resources

How many times have you said, "When I have X, I'll be able to do Y?" You don't need X to move forward. You need to just move. Stop getting stuck in analysis paralysis. Stop letting your environment stifle your creativity. Stop lamenting your lack of support. Instead, carve out a space to let your mind think and dream of the impossible. Build a mastermind or support posse of people who root for your success. And most of all, realize that the only resource you need is your mind. How can you foster your creative mind and encourage out-of-the-box thinking?

4. Understand the Motivation Factor

A lack of motivation is really a lack of clarity. If you don't know where you want to go, it's hard to see how to get there. Make a list of the last five things you accomplished, then take a moment to celebrate those wins. Give yourself a much-needed pat on the back. Then write down five new beliefs about yourself (I can do hard things; I figure out solutions, etc.).

5. Realign Your Viewpoint

Who do you want to be? That can be a tough question, but if you give yourself space and time to think about it, you can come up with the answer. Do you want to be athletic? Wealthy? Generous? Do you want to do philanthropic things? Realign your viewpoint on who you are and who you want to be. Write down that vision of yourself.

6. Set Far-Out Goals

Now it's time to set those C-goals. Dream big and dream things that seem impossible. Close your eyes and picture something so amazing that you get emotional just thinking about it. Imagine the new you that you just dreamed of in this incredible future. What are you doing? What are you wearing? Who is with you? Where do you live? What do you do day to day?

Once you've dreamed of the goal, you have to start trusting that the Universe has got it. You don't have to worry about the "how." Just concern yourself with the "what." Write down this goal in the present tense: *I am so grateful I . . . . I am living . . . . I am . . . .* Keep it on a card that you read every day, multiple times a day. Recite it in your head often.

7. Build the Mission

Use the 3-3-3 exercise to start building the intentional action steps for reaching your goal. Make a list of all the ways you can achieve the goal. Nothing is too outlandish or crazy. Give yourself plenty of creative mental space, and if you need to, complete this exercise over a few days. Keep making a list and then when you have exhausted your imagination, choose two actionable items from that list and make them your next to-dos.

8. Create Mental Kevlar

Remember the six keys to mental Kevlar when things get tough: Imagination, Will, Perception, Intuition, Memory, and Reason. Now, imagine you have achieved this amazing goal. Hold that vision in your head with your willpower. Recognize where you may be perceiving something incorrectly, and then trust your intuition. Focus on positive memories of past achievements and use the power of reason to see that if you have been successful in the past, you can be again. Now, go back to that vision and spend time each day seeing it on a projection screen in your head as if it has already happened.

9. Know Who Is the Real Problem

Very often, the biggest roadblock to success is staring back at you in the mirror. We self-sabotage, undermine, and slip back into our old paradigms and negative patterns. Look at what you are telling yourself on a daily basis. Are you filling your cup with joy, gratitude, and humility, or is it chock-full of harsh words, fears, and complaints? Because you choose what is in your cup, and if you choose negativity, that will come out whenever you hit a setback. Write out several positive affirmation statements and reread them throughout your day.

10. Create an Attitude of Success

Think about a situation that's not going well, something that you want to improve, and write it down on a piece of paper in as much detail as possible. Write three columns (or draw a stick figure) of your *Thoughts, Feelings,* and *Actions.* Write down your thoughts about the situation, what feelings come up, and what actions you have taken up to this point. Is this all working for you? If not, what new thoughts, feelings, and actions can you come up with?

11. Form a Foundation of Core Values

We talked about who you wanted to be while realigning your viewpoint. Now it's time to see if your core values are being honored or forgotten. Go back to that image of the person you want to be. Are you acting like that person every day? Or are there new habits you can implement that will build you into that person? Write down a list of new habits and the results you will see. Now take one step every single day in that direction.

12. Continue to Refill the Well

You must continue refilling the well with positive thinking, creativity, and new habits if you want to stop yourself from slipping back into those old paradigms. Check out my podcast, blog posts, or free downloads at stretchintosuccess.com/ratracereboot, or book a call with me to find out how you can take the next step toward the life of your dreams.

I want you to have that life you envisioned in the very beginning. It is possible—if you can change the one thing that is holding you back: your mind. Everything is created twice, remember. Once in your imagination (in your mind) and once in physical form. But you have to believe it is achievable for it to go from imagined to real.

Write to me and let me know how you escaped the rat race and how you are rebooting your life to become the one you dreamed of. Then take all that positive energy and use it to help the next person find their dreams!

Download my workbook to put all those dreams on paper and start taking that next step today!

ABOUT THE AUTHOR

Laura Noel is an Organizational Development consultant, leadership coach, and a senior consultant and facilitator with The Arbinger Institute. Prior to launching her business, Stretch Into Success, Laura served in the United States Air Force for more than 27 years, rising to the rank of Chief Master Sergeant. She spent much of her Air Force career teaching personal growth and leadership, most recently as the Commandant for the Joint Base Pearl Harbor-Hickam Noncommissioned Officer Academy, leading a team of nine instructors responsible for teaching leadership development and management skills to 392 students annually.

Since retiring from the Air Force, Laura has served as a consultant to organizations, individuals, and solopreneurs to streamline business processes while maximizing effectiveness, alignment, and impact. She helps clients stretch their thinking and minds in a way that opens them up to new possibilities.

Laura is a PsyD candidate in the field of Leadership Psychology and Neuroscience at William James College, where she serves as adjunct faculty. She has continued to develop her expertise as a coach and consultant through her studies. She also worked closely with her mentor, the late Bob Proctor, for years. Proctor was a world-renowned expert in human potential and success.

Laura has spent several years singing professionally in the USAF Band, both throughout the Boston area and around the world. When she's not helping clients improve their results, you can probably find her working on her music. She is married to her best friend and fellow Airman, Gary. They have two pups, Luna and Jasper.

www.ingramcontent.com/pod-product-compliance
Lightning Source LLC
Chambersburg PA
CBHW051519120626
46551CB00012B/994